WORTES AND ALL: MEDIEVAL COOKING

EMMA KAY

For Nick and Ben

First published 2025

Amberley Publishing
The Hill, Stroud,
Gloucestershire, GL5 4EP

www.amberley-books.com

ISBN: 978 1 3981 1099 1 (print)
ISBN: 978 1 3981 1100 4 (ebook)

British Library Cataloguing in Publication Data.
A catalogue record for this book is available from the British Library.

Typeset in 10pt on 13pt Celeste.
Origination by Amberley Publishing.
Printed in the UK.

Appointed GPSR EU Representative: Easy Access System Europe Oü, 16879218
Address: Mustamäe tee 50, 10621, Tallinn, Estonia
Contact Details: gpsr.requests@easproject.com, +358 40 500 3575

Contents

Introduction 4

1 Soups, Stews, Breads and Dough 7

2 Meat, Fish and Sauces 28

3 Dairy, Eggs, Fruit and Veg 48

4 Sweet Treats and Drinks 66

Notes 89

Bibliography 94

Introduction

The medieval period extends from the end of Roman occupation in the fifth century up until the beginning of the sixteenth century. It is a long and significant period in British history and held immense social and economic change. The early part of the medieval period was dominated by Germanic and Scandinavian influences until the Norman Conquest of 1066 when England shifted from Pagan to Christian belief systems. Castle culture and feudal land practices were prominent at this time, which also marked a turning point in democracy with the Magna Carta. Later years were dominated by war and plague, culminating in the rise of the Tudor dynasty in the late fifteenth century. All this in one era. As you can imagine, the evolution of food and drink within this period of significant change was diverse and progressive, depending on your place in society of course.

Contrary to outmoded theories, there really was no 'Dark Age', other than the fact that most people were illiterate. There is plenty of evidence to suggest that the British Isles was a thriving territory, trading widely and exchanging goods like for like across the Mediterranean. Continental pottery, European glassware, spices, dried exotic fruits, oils, and garlic bulbs to name just a few have all been discovered in various sites from Lancashire, London and Suffolk to Oxford and Cornwall, dating anywhere from the fifth to the tenth centuries. Early medieval leechdoms, or medicinal tomes, like those transcribed by the nineteenth-century scholar Oswald Cockayne also make frequent references to pepper, ginger, cumin and cinnamon and hint at communities having access to broad cooking techniques and ingredients.

Most of the research sources for determining the culinary background to this epoch are manuscripts opposed to books, which emerged gradually towards the end of the medieval era. The recipes found in both of these categories are more like lists, with scant methods than actual cooking instructions, often written in Latin or Old/Middle English which adds to the chaos.

In the houses of the noble and wealthy, meals of the Middle Ages could be quite ceremonial and there was a level of protocol. The seating of each guest was carefully thought out, while items like the table salt were positioned closest to the most important attendees, the formality of which reflected the old Anglo-Saxon mead hall customs of the early medieval age, with its orderly cup bearing etiquette. Light evening suppers complemented a significant midday meal. Breakfasts were not favoured in the medieval period, although it was customary to break your fast following a long night's sleep with a morsel of bread and something to drink in the morning.

Most communities of the Middle Ages lived rurally, with peasants working the land for whoever owned it, be it lord, institute of learning or monastery. Serfs were owned by the landowner, while freemen could rent land and make their own money from it.

The majority of people were not literate and lived by very meagre means, and it is easy to forget when researching this period that most of the dishes that were written down would only have been eaten by a very small section of wealthy and elite society. Our understanding is therefore very skewed about the eating and drinking habits of the everyday person living in the Middle Ages. Any information documented about the poor is also biased and from the perspective of the writer. Some of the best sources of research can be found in the records of poor relief. The accounts of almshouses suggest that porridges of grains and peas were eaten frequently, along with purchases of butter and salt. St Anthony's Hospital in London documents cooked oatmeal or peas and onions and flounders, interspersed with mutton, pork and fish. In contrast, the staff were provided with chickens, eels, crabs, oysters, apples, pears and wine.

Replica medieval cookware.
(© Emma Kay)

Many standard living spaces comprised of a single room with a central fire, which heated the space as well as offering a basic cooking facility. Those with greater status often had a separate kitchen in a building detached from the house itself (to minimise fires and odours) and there would be separate areas for the dairy, brewhouse, a pantry to store meat and so on. Towards the end of the medieval period kitchens were being integrated into the main property – sometimes at the end of the dining hall itself.

Central to the kitchen of the gentry would be a stone hearth, which would sometimes big enough for several people to sleep in. Spits and pots would be suspended over the fire and often clay ovens for bread and pastries would accompany the main hearth. In royal households and as the medieval period wore on, separate pastry kitchens and sometimes boiling houses for meats, fish and soup/stews were built close to the main kitchen.

The types of utensils and cooking equipment used changed little throughout the Middle Ages. If you were poor, a one-pot option like a cauldron was typical. For the wealthy there would be numerous sized copper pans, bronze and earthenware cooking vessels and three-legged posnets, skillets and trivets, which were sometimes known as brandreths, placed in the fire with the cooking vessel on top. Nothing really that dissimilar to today really.

Food was generally eaten with the fingers; there were no forks. Knives were necessary for cutting meat and pewter spoons were central to wealthier households, or wooden if you were less affluent.

This book, which categorises food and drink from the early medieval period between the fourth and thirteenth centuries and later medieval periods from the fourteenth to sixteenth centuries, merely provides a snapshot of eating and drinking during this time. It is by no means a definitive study. I suggest you consult books by authors such as Peter Brears, Constance Hieatt, Debby Banham, Laura Mason, Glyn Hughes, Peter Hammond, Maggie Black for a much more comprehensive overview of this vast culinary era.

1

Soups, Stews, Breads and Dough

Soups and Stews

Early Medieval

Stone tablets from the region of Mesopotamia belonging to Yale University's Babylonian Collection have been identified as the oldest-known recipes in the world. Three of these tablets are circa 1730 BC, equivalent to the Stone or Early Bronze Age. One tablet lists the ingredients for twenty-five different stews and broths. The most popular supplementary ingredients for almost all the recipes include leeks, onions and garlic, while cumin, coriander, mint and juniper berries are mentioned with regularity. The tablets also impart intricate cooking instructions including vocabulary for mixing, slicing, squeezing, shredding, crumbing, straining and filtering. It isn't unfeasible to imagine that communities living in the British Isles may well have been using these same techniques.

Soups and stews are staple ancient dishes that would often have been paired with bread to provide a basic form of sustenance in the absence of potatoes.

While the word 'soup' is a fairly modern one derived from both the Old English *supan* and Old French *souppe*, the word 'stew' originates from the Roman vivaria fishponds, which were later known as 'stews' or places where fish were kept for eating.

Although historians are divided as to how much the Romans influenced everyday customs and practices of those living in England at this time, the Roman culinary manuscript De Re Coquinaria (more commonly known as *Apicius*, after its alleged author) offers insight into the types of food that may have been consumed by the elite in England during the Roman occupation. One such example is this translated recipe for barley broth:

Barley Broth

Crush well washed barley, soaked the day before, place on the fire to be cooked. When hot add plenty of it, a small bunch of dill, dry onion, satury and colocasium, (possibly a type of bean) to be cooked together because this gives a better juice; add green coriander and a little salt; bring it to a boiling point. When well heated take out the bunch dill and transfer the barley into another vessel to avoid burning on the bottom

Cuneiform text containing culinary recipes, Old Babylonian period (*c.* 1900–1600 BCE). (Museum No. YBC 4644, CC BY-SA 4.0)

Roman vivarium.

of the pot; thin it out with water, broth, milk and strain into a pot, covering the tips of the colocasia. Next crush pepper, lovage, a little dry flea-bane, cumin and sylphium, stir well, add vinegar, reduced must and broth; put it back in the pot; the remaining colocasia finish on a gentle fire.[1]

It's probable that these Romanic combinations and techniques dictated future recipes, together with the impact that Germanic, Scandinavian, Middle Eastern and French-Norman occupations contributed. Certainly, before there were medieval broths and pottages, there were Anglo-Saxon *brops* and *briws*. Despite there being few recorded actual recipes of any kind before the eleventh century in England, the early medieval 'leechdoms', or remedies recorded prior to the Norman Conquest and famously translated by the Victorian scholar Oswald Cockayne, offer an insight into how broths were prepared for medicinal purposes. For hiccups, known then as hickets, a broth made of mint, carrot, cumin or ginger was recommended. There are other more elaborate medicinal broths, like one containing vinegar, meat, herbs, peas, leeks and cheese soaked in goats' milk to be served to anyone suffering from dysentery, as well as a bean broth for liver disease, while a combination of pig meat, beets, mallow and brassica or nettles seeped in salted water could also do wonders for constipation apparently.

Eleventh to Thirteenth Centuries

The *briws* and *brops* of the centuries before evolved somewhat predictably with the onset of Norman rule into pottages, from the Old French word *potage*.

St Hildegard of Bingen was born in Germany towards the very end of the eleventh century. She wrote a seminal text, *Physica*, reflecting the medicinal treatments of the day,

A spread of Roman foods. (© Emma Kay)

A cook at the hearth with his ladle. (Woodcut from the first printed cookbook in German, *Kuchenmaistrey*)

A scene from the Bayeux Tapestry depicting Bishop Odo rallying Duke William's troops during the Battle of Hastings in 1066.

which, like the leeches, offer additional information relating to basic cooking techniques and the relationship between food and health. As with most societies of this era there was a strong belief system for ensuring both humors and elements remained balanced throughout the body in order to maintain general wellness. The four humors were: blood (the air element), being hot and moist; phlegm (the water element), which is cold and moist; yellow bile (the fire element), which is hot and dry; and black bile, or the earth element, which is cold and dry. The humors were also linked to psychological wellbeing and temperament, which meant some sweet foods were seen as hot and moist, while sharp and tart foods were considered cold and dry. So if your temperament was cold and moist (i.e. phlegmatic), there would be a need to eat hot and dry foods like garlic, pepper or onions, whereas a hot and tempestuous (or choleric) temperament required the consumption of produce like fresh and cool cucumbers or spinach and so on.

As a nun and abbess, Hildegard would have worked hard to ensure the monastery she was responsible for produced a good year-round mix of herbs and arable crops to sustain everyone, but I certainly wouldn't advocate her soup recipe to alleviate muscular issues.

> **Titmouse** [For anyone wondering, this is a bird and not a rodent]
> The titmouse is hot and dry. It is tame, flies in clear air, has healthy flesh and is good for both sick and well people to eat. A person who is troubled by palsy should cook titmouse in water, with butter, and make soup from it. He should eat this frequently, and he will be cured.[2]

Above left: Hildegard of Bingen.

Above right: The four humors in relation to the four elements and their zodiac signs. (Woodcut from Quinta Essentia, Leipzig)

Medieval titmouse.

It is imperative to recognise the influence that Middle and Near Eastern societies had across Europe during the medieval period by way of trade, occupation and cultural exchange. We know that migrant farmers from Turkish, Syrian, and other neighbouring countries probably crossed the English Channel as early as the Neolithic age, introducing sheep into the British Isles. By the medieval period Mediterranean and Arabic culture had pervaded most communities.

One of the earliest known Arabic cookery collations, *Kitab al-Ṭabīḫ*, initially forged in the tenth century by the Baghdadi author Ibn Sayyār Al-Warrāq, would have been known to literate society and retained in some of the great private libraries of the age. It is replete with ancient recipes for stews, some of which must undoubtedly have influenced the grander kitchens of Europe.

Muslim armies occupying Spain in the 700s cultivated rice there. When exactly rice came across to England is debatable, but it certainly appears in recipes of the fourteenth century, most notably the *Forme of Cury*, a compilation of recipes allegedly put together by the cooks of King Richard II.

The following recipe for stew containing rice to relieve gastric ailments is taken from *Kitab al-Ṭabīḫ*.

A Stew for upset stomachs

Start with unhusked rice, dry toast it in a frying pan and remove whatever is shelled of its husk. Then boil the rice with pomegranate seeds [and water]. When it is done, add a piece of long pepper (darfulful), a small piece of ginger, salt and cumin, all ground.

Continue boiling until everything is cooked. Let the final stew be thin so that the sick person can sip it (yahsu). It is good for indigestion and for those whose food lingers in the stomach undigested. It purges flatulence and softens and improves the bowels. It is quite healthy and easy to digest. God Willing.[3]

Spices and creating big flavours were of paramount importance to medieval cooks and English recipes of this period borrowed heavily from the early Middle Eastern manuscripts, incorporating almonds in the form of oil, milk, flour, pomegranates, exotic spices, broths with rice, honey, rose water, sugar and eggs, like this recipe from the manuscript Arundel 334 (after Thomas Arundel), found within the collections of the Bodleian Library and *c.* 1425. It is translated here by the late medieval scholar Constance Hieatt:

> **Rice Lombard**
> Take rice and pick them [the grains] clean and wash them, and parboil them, and put them in a pot; add good beef broth and sugar or honey and let it boil, and colour it with saffron; and if you want to have it very thick, take raw egg yolks and beat them well together, and draw them well together, and draw them through a strainer, and put it in the pot and let it boil with the pottage, and then arrange it in dishes and take hard egg yolks and cloves and maces and minced ginger, and mix them together, and strew on top, and serve it forth.[4]

Late Medieval

The Canterbury Tales, written by Geoffrey Chaucer in the fourteenth century, offers some observations of earlier medieval food and drink via the narratives of his famous pilgrims. He mentions the cook's ability to make 'good stews and soup, and tasty pies', although this image is swiftly ruined with Chaucer's mischievous reference to the cook's open fetid sores. Chaucer also mentions 'mortrewes' of which there were two types: a soup made of meats like chicken or pork with breadcrumbs, egg yolks and saffron, or an alternative fish-based mortrewes of fish offal or roe, bread and ale. Both sets of ingredients were mashed down in a mortar, hence the name, to form the soup itself.[5] The mortrewes/mortrews recipe I have chosen here is taken from the lyrical recipes contained in *Liber Cure Cocorum* of 1430, translated in the nineteenth century by Richard Norris.

Rice Lombard. (© Emma Kay)

The cook from Chaucer's *Canterbury Tales*. (From Ellesmere manuscripts *c*. 1410, Huntington Library, California)

Mortrews of Flesh.
Take hens and fresh pork, I teach you,
Seethe them together always then;
Take them up, pick out the bones,
Slice thin the pork,Sir, for the nonys;
Hew it small and grind it well,
Cast it again, so have you bliss,
Into the broth, and thicken it then
With grated wastel [bread], as I teach you;
Color it with saffron, at that time;
Boil it and set it down to one side;
Mix it with yolks of eggs right,
And garnish your dish with [spice] powder you might.[6]

Herbelade/Erbolate appears in manuscripts of the fourteenth and fifteenth centuries and is described in John Russell's *Boke of Nature* as 'a liquor of boiled lard and herbs, mixed with dates, currants, and Pynez, (pinenuts) strained, sugared, coloured, whipped, & put into fayre round cofyns of almondes for states fulle dewe'.[7]

Herbolades appear to be the same the century before, as described in the *Forme of Cury*. Their purpose serves as a basic meat stock, which was added to the contents of various pies and savoury tarts.

Bread and Dough

Early Medieval

As early as the Neolithic era communities were farming ancient grains like emmer, einkorn, and barley while the 'common bread wheat' with a higher gluten content, which we are most familiar with today, was arguably first introduced by the Romans. Bronze

Einkorn.

Age communities of the British Isles were also enjoying spelt from the Middle East, an adaptable grain that stored well, and the cultivation of beans and peas undoubtedly would have promoted all kinds of new flours ground down on granite saddle querns. Giant storage pits have been unearthed all over Britain. These deep pits were cut into bedrock and filled. Their function was to protect crop seeds, ensuring they weren't damaged or didn't germinate too early.

The Old English word for bread is *breadru,* which may have its origins in Latin or derive from the Gothic word *broe,* meaning to brew. Some breadmaking did, after all, rely on the yeasts formed during brewing. The phrase *half-maesse,* or loaf mass, is most associated with the August Anglo-Saxon festival of Lammas, adopted after the country's conversion to Christianity, although its origins as a former pagan festival remain a possibility. Bread was blessed in harmony with the harvests during Lammas. Historian Eleanor Parker suggests Lammas bread could have acted as the Eucharist (Holy Communion), perhaps even being made out of the first harvested wheat.[8] Lammas is undoubtedly linked to the modern-day harvest festivals of Thanksgiving, held in October. The traditionally curious-shaped loaves offered up by the community are reminiscent of this. It's possible Anglo-Saxons commemorated Lammas with a specialist shaped ceremonial loaf, similar to festival and ritual breads eaten by the Romans.

Eleventh to Thirteenth Centuries

Although some medieval breads remained unleavened, raised loaves have been crafted since ancient times, as soon as the concept of natural airborne yeasts were harnessed, and leavening sourdoughs were reserved to leaven the next batch.

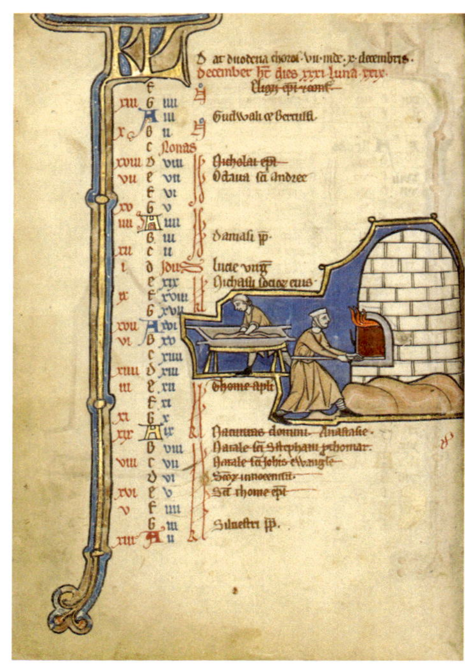

Above left: Spelt.

Above right: Detail of baking bread in a psalter by an unknown illuminator, Belgium, mid-1200s. Tempera colours, gold leaf and ink on parchment, each leaf 9¼ × 6½ in. (J. Paul Getty Museum, ms. 14, fol. 8v)

Flatbreads. (© Emma Kay)

Sourdough starter.
(© Emma Kay)

Regimen sanitatis Salerni [Regiment of Health] advocated the following advice on the preparation and eating of bread in the twelfth century:

> Bread should be neither warm nor stale.
> It should be leavened, raised, well-baked.
> Moderately salted, and chosen from the best grains.
> Do not eat the crust since it causes burning choler.
> Bread that is salted, leavened, well-baked,
> Pure, and healthy should be of great benefit to you.[9]

Some of the best resources relating to earlier medieval food and drink of the British Isles can be found in monastic records. Monks worked round the clock in the bakehouses of early monasteries, where bread was both ceremonial and integral to their diet, with the dough prepared from the natural yeasts formed in the beer brewing process.

On feast days, and there were many – some sixty odd in fact throughout the medieval Christian calendar – Benedictine monks were allocated a 'pittance', which was a better-quality bread, opposed to the dark and heavy everyday rye-based doughs. Introduced by the Anglo-Saxons, rye was a useful grain as it could be grown in all conditions and most terrain.

Bread has always been an integral part of global religious ceremonies. The Armenian Gata pastry/bread was traditionally consumed during Candlemas and even sold outside monasteries. One of the trademarks of this ancient bread are the ornamental patterns it is decorated with. Both Stone and Bronze Age examples of the stamps used to emboss Gata have been unearthed in Armenia and its neighbouring regions, leading to the theory that these markings were part of a ritual sacrifice to individual deities. Bread stamps and cookie moulds formed an important relationship with baked products throughout medieval Europe, from animals, plants and people to religious symbols. From Roman bread stamps bearing the name of the maker to initialling loaves and pies to identify them for the communal bakehouses once found in every town and village. Think of that old nursery rhyme line: 'Roll it, pat it and mark it with a B. Throw it in the oven for baby and me.'

Just as estate lords would often 'pay' their farmworkers in food in accordance with the medieval feudal system, the monks were obliged to regularly feed weary travellers

Scene from *Regimen sanitatis salernitanum*.

Medieval monk baking bread.

Armenian Gata pastry stand outside of Geghard Monastery. (Courtesy of Rita Willaert, CC BY 2.0)

or destitute members of their parish. Many of their own tenant farmers were also richly rewarded. The abbot of Titchfield supplied his workers with two daily meals of meat or fish and bread and ale, cider and broth. The tenants were then provided with a supper of fish together with a 40 oz (just over 100 g) of wheat loaf, which rotated as a barley loaf on consecutive days. This was a luxury, considering rye bread was a more typical contribution. Each manor and what they provided their tenants varied widely. In 1291 tenants working the land at the manor of Broughton downed tools and went on strike, complaining that the loaves they were supplied with were not large enough, a case they later lost in court.[10]

Late Medieval

The catastrophic series of crop failures throughout the 1300s impacted dramatically on the diets of everyone across Britain and wider Europe, but particularly poorer people, as the price of grains soared and the eventual absence of all foods drove people to criminal acts. In fourteenth-century Norfolk alone, crimes rose by 382 per cent compared to pre-famine years.[11] Communities turned to meat opposed to cereal-based foods and there were even some accounts of people eating dogs and carrion, as well as resorting to cannibalism in Europe, including England, at this time.[12]

Cockel/cockle bread is largely connected with the seventeenth century, although its origins are perhaps much older. It is referenced in Harley MS 2378, a miscellany of medicinal and culinary texts dating primarily to the fifteenth century but added to into the early part of the 1700s.[13] It has numerous associations, one of which refers to the flour for the bread itself, mixed with cockle-weed. It also has sexual connotations, being linked to a lascivious dance involving women lifting their skirts, clambering onto a table and moving their knees in an action replicating the kneading of dough.

> My dame is sick and gone to bed,
> And I'll go mould my cockle-bread:
> Up with my heels and down with my head
> And this is the way to mould cockle-bread.[14]

Medieval feudalism.

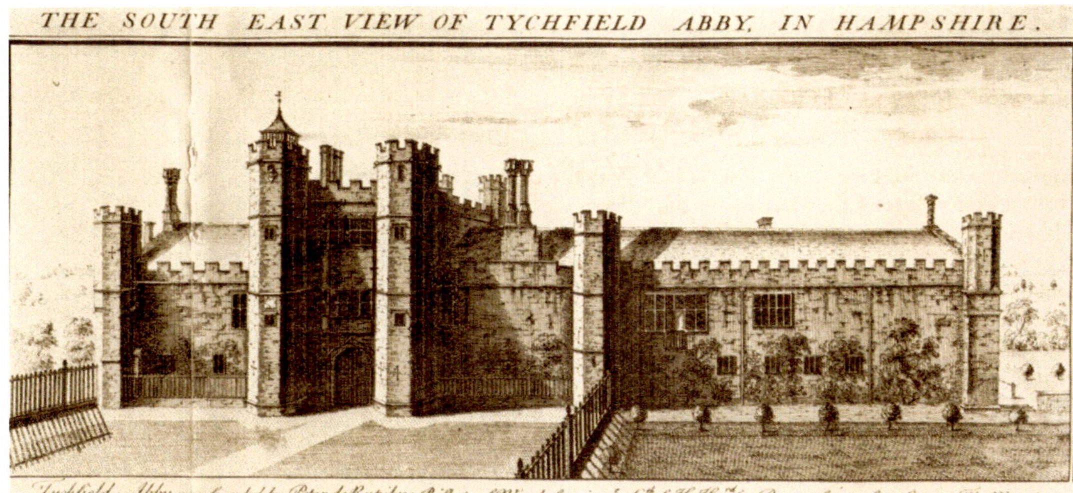

Titchfield Abbey.

The Apocalypse in a *Biblia Pauperum* illuminated at Erfurt around the time of the Great Famine. Death sits astride a manticore whose long tail ends in a ball of flame (Hell). Famine points to her hungry mouth.

After preparing the dough it was pressed into the private parts, baked and served up to the object of the woman's affections.

This strange charade is also associated with the medieval game of hot-cockles, which became firmly established by the nineteenth century.[15]

The word cockle, of course, may be reminiscent of the French *coquille,* a shell, typically the scallop shell – a scallop and the shape of a vulva do bear similarities.

John Russell's *Boke of Nurture* provides detailed information relating to fifteenth-century manners, behaviour, the duties of servants and table serving among other activities related to historic courtesy. Of bread, Russell advised:

> Give your Sovereign new bread,
> alwey thy soueraynes bred thow choppe, & þat it be newe & able;
> others one-day-old bread;
> se all*e* oþ*er* bred a day old or þou choppe to þe table;
> for the house, three-day bread;
> all*e* howsold bred iij. dayes old / so it is p*ro*fitable;
> for trenchers four-day bread;
> trencher bred iiii. dayes is co*n*venyent & agreable.[16]

A trencher, of the recommended four-day-old variety, was a round and flat hollowed out piece of hard, stale bread used to serve food. It was also an edible plate that could be recycled after dinner with the remains of any sauce or leftovers to mop up. Maguelonne Toussaint-Samat proposes that the wealthier sorts did not eat their trenchers, preferring to feed them to eager dogs or the poorer echelons of society lurking outside in the streets.[17] Many people, like Toussaint-Samat, cite the onset of the Renaissance with the replacement of plates, although Russell, writing well into the fifteenth century, suggests otherwise. Certainly, by the late 1600s pewter or silver trenchers would have been a typical feature on the dinner tables of the wealthy. English cook William Rabisher mentions bread trenchers as late as 1675 in his book *The Whole Body of Cookery.*[18]

Hollow trencher. (© Emma Kay)

Another quirky type of bread, listed simply as 'cruste rolles' and clearly more of a tortilla than an actual bread roll, makes an appearance in Thomas Austin's reproduced manuscripts of the 1400s, published in 1888 under the title *Two Fifteenth-Century Cookery-Books*.

> **Cruste Rolle**
> Take fayre smal Flowre of whete; nym Eyroun & breke þer-to, & coloure þe past with Safroun; rolle it on a borde also þinne as parchement, rounde a-bowte as an oblye;*. [Oble, sacramental wafer] frye hem, & serue forth; and þus may do in lente, but do away þe Eyroun, & nym mylke of Almaundys, & frye hem in Oyle, & þen serue forth.[19]

The following is my own translation, followed by my reworked version:

> Take wheat flour and eggs, mix together and colour with some saffron. Roll the dough out as thin as parchment paper and cut into rounds like sacramental wafers (communion wafers). Fry them and serve forth. During Lent the eggs can be substituted with almond milk.

Medieval Wheat Tortillas (makes around 25 or 35 if rolled very thin)

240 g strong white flour
1 egg beaten
½ teaspoon salt
½ teaspoon baking powder

About 6 strands of saffron left to infuse in 90 ml water.
10 ml olive oil
Vegetable oil for frying

- Start by leaving the saffron strands to infuse in the water either for a couple of hours or overnight to achieve a lovely vibrant orangery-red liquid.
- Combine flour, salt and baking powder.
- Make a well in the centre and add the infused water (saffron strands and all), olive oil and the beaten egg. Mix together with your hands to reach a smooth paste. If it's too runny, add a little more flour; too dense, add a little more water. You want a fairly pliable dough.
- Turn the dough mix onto a floured board and knead for a minute or two until silky.
- Roll the dough out and, using a 15 cm round cutter (I actually used a small mixing bowl), cut individual circles. If you want a nacho consistency, roll your dough nice and thin. I made more of a fried tortilla bread, so the dough was a couple of cm thick.
- Cut each circle into 4 wedges, like you might cut a pie. Place all the cut wedges onto some baking parchment and set aside.
- Heat the pan with the vegetable oil. Make sure you use enough to cover the tortillas in frying.
- Turn the heat up high and add the tortillas in batches. They will only take about 2 minutes. Make sure you turn them to brown both sides.
- Using a slotted spoon place the tortillas onto a plate lined with some kitchen roll. Quickly add some sea salt or rock salt.
- These are great eaten either warm or cold and are good for dipping or as a side dish.

Recreation of medieval tortillas (cruste rolle).
(© Emma Kay)

A wastel was a type of superior fine wheat bread, similar to simnel and other ceremonial loaves. An interesting recipe for Wastels Yfarced (stuffed wastel bread) appears in the *Forme of Cury*:

> **Wastels Yfarced**
> Take a Wastel and hewe out þe crummes. take ayrenn & shepis talow & þe crummes of þe same Wastell powdour fort & salt with Safroun and Raisouns coraunce. & medle alle þise yfere & do it in þe Wastel. close it & bynde it fast togidre. and seeþ it wel.[20]

Here's my own translation:

> Take a wastel loaf and scoop out the crumbs. Take eggs and mutton suet and mix with the crumbs from the wastel. Add salt and saffron, raisins/currants and blend together. Stuff it back into the hollowed-out loaf. Close it together and boil it well.

Similar to wastel, manchet bread was made with very fine, good-quality flour. Mayne was a word sometimes applied to something of good quality, while cheet or cheat/chett bread was bread prepared with a lower quality of flour. If you purchased a manchet but actually received an inferior cheet loaf, you had obviously been cheated a crime that was punishable by being publicly dragged through the streets.[21] Although there is another argument to suggest that 'cheat' simply meant loaf. Therefore, a 'mayne cheat' became a manchet. Both have a legacy that extends to the 1400s at least. There was also a superior bread termed payn(d)mayn. It is spelt in many different ways, but is often associated with Communion bread.

Medieval craknell/craknel recipes are diverse and include ones for boiling or baking. Sometimes they are likened to small cakes or other times as hard biscuits. There are also early references to them being baked twice. Essentially, I think they were meant to be crunchy, like their name implies. An early mention appears in 1400 in the accounts for Bristol, where the following law applied to local bakers: 'that to the feast of Easter ... none of them shall make Crakenelle in the town, which if they shall have done and been convicted thereof, so often as it shall happen that any one of them be convicted...'[22]

Medieval baking laws, or the assize of bread, is both complex and a bit tedious to relay, but it's safe to say this type of legislation was not uncommon. The Latin and Old English text in the British Library, known as MS 1735, compiled by the medical practitioner John Crophill around the late 1400s, contains a common recipe of the time combining eggs, broth and breadcrumbs, known as Jussele/Jussel/Jussell.

> Mye wastelbred swenge eyren & do ther to tak good fat broth of freysch beof colour it with saffron boille it al softely & in the boyllingg do al this ther to & do to sauge & percyle.[23]

This dish was sometimes served with a sweet, creamy sauce, but it is also reminiscent of a stuffing known to Anglo-Saxon communities used to stuff roasted meats and is still pertinent to modern-day cooking, as my own version below demonstrates and is absolutely delicious.

Medieval punishments for bakers.

Medieval bakers at work.

Rich Jussell for Stuffing

140 g brioche breadcrumbs
1 beaten egg
350/400 ml beef or meat broth
Pinch of saffron
20 g of fresh mixed chopped sage and parsley. Alternatively, you can substitute with a couple of teaspoons each of dried sage and parsley
Salt and pepper to taste

- Mix the breadcrumbs, sage and parsley and add the beaten eggs. Combine. Finally stir in the broth, season and let it cool.
- Heat your oven to 180°C / 350°F / gas mark 4.
- Grease a baking tray or dish, add the mixture and bake for around 20 minutes.
- Alternatively, you can stuff or roll your meat of choice with the stuffing and roast.

Recreation of jussell.
(© Emma Kay)

A quintessential medieval dish that remains familiar today is the rissole. Rissoles originally consisted of chopped meat or fruit rolled up in dough and fried. In fact, there were numerous filled parcels of cheese, meats and miscellaneous broth concoctions. Too many to include here.

This 1430 recipe translated from *Liber Cure Cocorum* mentions the phrase 'roller', which was a little-used Middle English term for a pastry crust. Some countries in Europe and further afield have their own variation of rissoles, many of which are fried in pastry or batter. In Britain, rissoles became an economical twentieth-century wartime favourite, replacing the dough with a breadcrumb coating.

For Rissoles
Take ground pork that has been seethed
With pepper and beaten eggs clean;
Put barm thereto, I undertake,
As light as [a] bubble it will it make;
Lay it in a roller as smelt fish,
Fry it in grease, lay it in dish.[24]

It's worth mentioning that bread was regularly gifted to the poor by parishes across Britain throughout the Middle Ages, on feast days and special occasions, or simply as alms bestowed upon the most destitute members of the community.

Recreation of medieval rissoles. (© Emma Kay)

2

Meat, Fish and Sauces

Meat and Fish

Early Medieval

Although no specific culinary recipes we would recognise today exist from this era in Britain, there are numerous references to cooking techniques applied to medicinal dishes, essentially prepared, cooked and eaten as meals, which were beneficial to people's health. As the leading researcher and translator of Anglo-Saxon leechdoms, Victorian scholar Oswald Cockayne's description of a typical feast, how it was hunted, caught, cooked and eaten, is authentically evocative of this early medieval era, so very incorrectly defined as the 'Dark Ages'.

> At his noon meat or dinner, at the *hora nona,* or ninth hour of the day, for the word noon has now changed its sense, the Saxon spread his table duly and suitably with a table cloth. He could place on it for the entertainment of his family and household, the flesh of neat cattle, now Normanized, as Sir Walter Scott has made familiar to all, into beef, the flesh of sheep, now called mutton, of pig of goat, of calf, of deer, especially the noble hart, of wild boar, the peacock, swan, duck, culver of pigeon, waterfowl, barndoor fowl, geese, and a great variety of wild fowl, which the fowler caught with net, noose, birdlime, birdcalls, hawks, and traps; salmons, eels, hake, pilchards, eelpouts, trout, lampreys, herrings, sturgeon, oysters, crabs, periwinkles, plaice, lobsters, sprats, and so on.
>
> The cookery of these viands was not wholly contemptible. It was entrusted to professors of that admired art, who could, through their accomplishments have been neglected by the annalists put on the board, oyster patties, and fowls stuffed with bread and such worts as parsley. Weaker stomachs could have light food, chickens, giblets, pigs trotters, eggs, broth, various preparations of mik ... From some of their drawings, their cookery of meat seems to have been more Homeric than Roman or modern English, for we see portions of meat brought up on small spits, all hot to the table. All food that required it was sweetened with honey...[1]

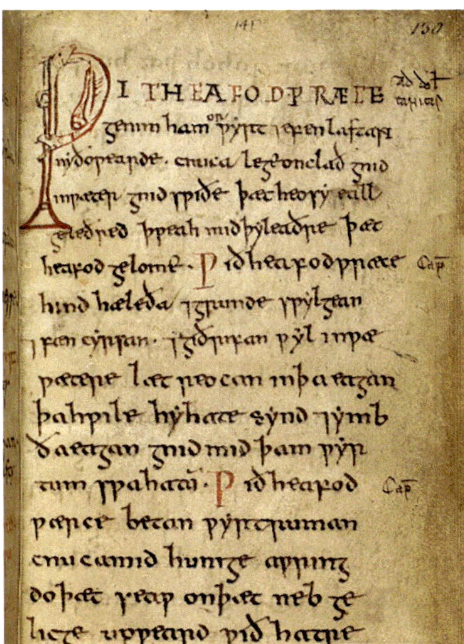

Lacnunga. (BL MS Harley, tenth or eleventh century)

Representation of Anglo-Saxon dining.

Cockayne was right. There are Anglo-Saxon documents, like Ælfric's Colloquy, which outline the importance of the role of bakers and describe the cooks as being integral to society at this time. Archaeological excavations also provide plenty of evidence of extensive fishing, particularly that of whales and porpoises, at sites such as the one in Flixborough, Lincolnshire, which revealed a large-scale cetacean fishery.[2] Grave remains have been discovered on the island of Lundy covered in limpet shells. The bodies are thought to be Viking and the shells were buried with them to take and eat in the afterlife.

The first cows in Britain were aurochs, which bore great long horns and were much larger than today's modern cattle. As they became more domesticated and integrated with different breeds from overseas the size, shape, colour and horn length of cows morphed from region to region over time. The red Sussex is one breed thought to descend from cows inhabiting England at the time of the Norman invasion.[3]

Sheep were introduced into the British Isles from the Near East sometime during the Neolithic era. And pigs, unlike our curly tailed pink variety today, were bristly tusked

Porpoise painted in the Middle Ages.

Early manuscript illustration of an aurochs.

Early manuscript illustration of a sheep.

native wild boars. In countries including Germany and the Netherlands the pig represents a symbol of good luck, and it is still customary to exchange pigs made of marzipan around New Year's Eve in Germany. I'm convinced this links into the old Anglo-Saxon tradition of holding the wild boar in high esteem. An extract from the Old Norse sagas, known as Edda, contains a story relating to Valhalla. It describes the first meal consumed after a warrior's death. In the saga a cook named Andhrimnir prepared 'Sæhrimnir' every night in his mighty cooking pot to satisfy all the new souls entering Valhalla. Sæhrimnir, the wild boar, is christened 'the best of flesh' as the pig represented both strength and fertility in Scandinavian cultures. Pig meat was the food of choice during mid-winter feasts, which we think of as Yule today, but was actually spelt more like 'geol'. These pigs were sacrificed and eaten as part of the wider Yule festivities which also included the ceremony of Heitstrenging – the making of a solemn vow to the pagan god Freyr, made against the bristles of the boar itself. In Sweden this tradition has been kept alive with the annual baking of the ginger biscuits Pepparkakor, often cut into pig shapes, a practice which merges the old Yule customs with the Christian festival of Christmas.

In the early medieval period the boar was so revered that it was crafted in metal to adorn helmets which would be buried with other important belongings beside the body. The best example of this is the Guilden Morden Boar, originating from around the seventh century, discovered in Cambridgeshire and thought to have been part of a Scandinavian boar-crested helmet. It is a misconception to think rabbits were imported by the Romans and established by the Normans, as evidence of their existence in areas like north-west Kent date back to the Stone Age at least. Hares, also associated with the Roman era, are mentioned in Cockayne's tenth-century leechdoms, their offal used in medicinal broths.[4]

Chickens may have been an Iron Age addition, brought from Asia via Europe, but there were certainly no turkeys around until the 1500s.

Roe and red deer were hunted on foot or by adopting the 'bow and stable' technique of herding animals into an enclosure and shooting them with arrows.[5] Anglo-Saxons also used large dogs to hunt stags and deer, boars, hares and goats.[6]

More exotic meat, like peacock, swan and duck, were consumed but considered unsuitable for the digestive system.[7] Although, if it had wings and a pulse, many varieties of bird were always an edible option.

It would have been typical to roast joints of meat or boil them for broths and stews on spits, cauldrons or pans over an open fire.

Meat was butchered in the autumn and preserved in salt, which has a mining heritage that extends at least to the Neolithic period in England. The flesh was likely to have been cured or soaked in brine. Alternatively, meat and fish could be air dried or smoked, the latter technique undoubtedly a contribution of the Vikings. Whole Viking era smoke houses have been excavated on sites like the one discovered at Granastaðir in north Iceland.

Eleventh to Thirteenth Centuries

The Muslim characteristics of Spanish occupation, which lasted a staggering 700 odd years, are reflected in an anonymous thirteent-century cookbook from Andalusia, with dishes like Mukhalal (now typically recognised in Arabic nations as pickled vegetables), but originally this involved cooking meats like beef, mutton or chicken in strong vinegar or Sanhâji, a sort of stew of everything from partridges and chicken to pigeons and meatballs often served at feasts.

Above: Fourteenth-century illustration showing the hunting of wild boar.

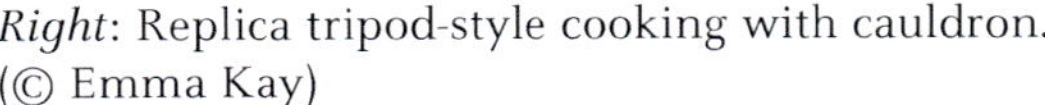

Right: Replica tripod-style cooking with cauldron. (© Emma Kay)

Herring drying in a modern dehydrator. (© Emma Kay)

Fish being smoked as the Vikings did. Royal Highland Show, 2018. (Courtesy of alljengi, CC BY-SA 2.0)

Manuscript illustrating Muslim rule in Spain.

Mukhallal

Take the meat of a plump cow or sheep, cut it small, and put it in a new pot with salt, pepper, coriander, cumin, plenty of saffron, garlic peeled and diced, almonds peeled and split, and plenty of oil; cover it with strong, very pure vinegar, without the slightest bit of water; put it on a moderate charcoal fire and stir it, then boil it. When it cooks and the meat softens and it reduces, then put it on the hearthstone and coat it with much egg, cinnamon and lavender; color it with plenty of saffron, as desired, and put in it whole egg yolks and leave it on the hearthstone until it thickens and the broth evaporates and the fat appears. This dish lasts many days without changing or spoiling; it is called 'wedding food' in the West [or the Algarve], and it is one of the seven dishes cited as used among us at banquets in Cordoba and Seville.[8]

Mirkâs, the Arabic name for an African lamb sausage, remains hugely popular today and is perhaps better known as a Merguez sausage in England and in France. Recipes like this that have altered slightly over time but bridge multiple communities historically, are testament to the tremendous legacy of medieval cooking.

Mirkâs (Merguez Sausage)

It is as nutritious as meatballs and since the pounding ripens it, makes it quick to digest, and it is good nutrition. First get some meat from the leg or shoulder of a lamb and pound it until it becomes like meatballs. Knead it in a bowl, mixing in some oil and some *murri naqi* (a sort of fermented barley paste), pepper, coriander seed, lavender, and cinnamon. Then add three quarters as much of fat, which should not be pounded, as it would melt with frying, but chopped up with a knife or beaten on a cutting board.

Merguez sausage. (Stu_spivack, Merguez, CC BY-SA 2.0)

> Using the instrument made for stuffing, stuff it in the washed gut, tied with thread to make sausages, small or large. Then fry them with some fresh oil and use it while hot. Some people make the sauce with the juice of cilantro and mint and some ground onion. Some cook it in a pot with oil and vinegar, some make it *râhibi* (like meatloaf) with onion and lots of oil until it is baked and browned. It is good whichever of these methods you use.[9]

One of the earliest documents describing the process of hunting and the consumption of food in mid-twelfth-century Europe is *Didascalicon,* a sort of early encyclopedia written by the Saxon canon Hugh of St Victor:

> Hunting is divided into gaming, fowling, and fishing.
> Gaming is done in many ways — with nets, foot-traps, snares,
> pits, the bow, javelins, the spear, encircling the game, or
> smoking it out, or pursuing it with dogs or hawks. Fowling is
> done by snares, traps, nets, the bow, birdlime, the hook.
> Fishing is done by drag-nets, lines, hooks, and spears. To this
> discipline belongs the preparation of all foods, seasonings, and
> drinks. Its name, however, is taken from only one part of it
> because in antiquity men used to eat merely by hunting, as they
> still do in certain regions where the use of bread is extremely
> rare, where flesh is the only food and water or mead the drink.
>
> Food is of two kinds — bread and side dishes...
> Side dishes consist of all that one eats with bread, and we can call them
> victuals. They are of many sorts — meats, stews, porridges,
> vegetables, fruits.
>
> Of meats, some are roasted, others fried,
> others boiled, some fresh, some salted. Some are called loins,
> flitches also or sides, haunches or hams, grease, lard, fat. The
> varieties of meat dishes are likewise numerous — Italian sausage,
> minced meat, patties, Galatian tarts, and all other such things
> that a very prince of cooks has been able to concoct.
>
> ...Hunting, therefore, includes all the duties of bakers, butchers,
> cooks, and tavern keepers.[10]

The British Isles were occupied by Normans, and therefore heavily influenced by their culture, until the middle of the twelfth century. Heralding from northern France, Normans represented the descendants of Frankish, Norse and Roman kinsmen and women. As a consequence, food and drink throughout this period became even more diverse. I think it's fair to say the Normans do tend to be credited with many dishes that were already known, however, though some medieval foods like brawne/braun/brawn are so generic that it's impossible to attach provenance.

Hugh of St Victor.

The earliest reference to this meaty ingredient appears alongside other food items in extracts of the 1375 account rolls for Durham Cathedral. In *liberacionibus Coquine ut supra* (In the deliverances of cooking) the list includes: 'suet, at a cost of 10d.; Brawne, 17d, figs 6d, almonds, 22d. 8 multon. sals., [a lot of salt] 4s. 8d.; a dozen doves from the manor of Billyngham, stuffing, 3s 2 cranes, 22d.; crayfish, 2s.; olei olive, 5s. 4d.'[11]

There are many conflicting medieval references to brawn, with citations ranging from the dark flesh of any animal including chickens and pigs to slices or, what were termed *leches* of meat, a boar or calf's head, a meat terrine made from the gelatinous outcomes of boiling an animal's head (usually a pig), which can be pressed into a mould, and so on. Then there's the original Old English definition, which literally just means broad or muscular. It's safe to say that whenever you do come across a reference for brawn, it will involve meat of some kind, and usually boar.

Late Medieval

The oldest known cookery book written in English, *The Forme of Cury* (cookery), dates to the end of the 1300s but was published by Simon Pegge in the 1700s. Pegge observed from the original manuscript that whole joints of meat were rarely eaten at the table at this time. Meat was instead cut into pieces, finely diced or ground down and added to soups, stews, ragouts and so on. By the sixteenth century it had become popular once again to serve spit-roasted joints at dinner time. If you were wealthy enough, this might include roast heron, swan or crane, or boiled whole chickens and poached fish. Dinner was the most important meal of the day, eaten around twelve noon, so more of a lunch than a dinner (depending on whether you reside in the north or the south of England), straddled between a basic breakfast and a meagre supper.

Durham Cathedral in the nineteenth century.

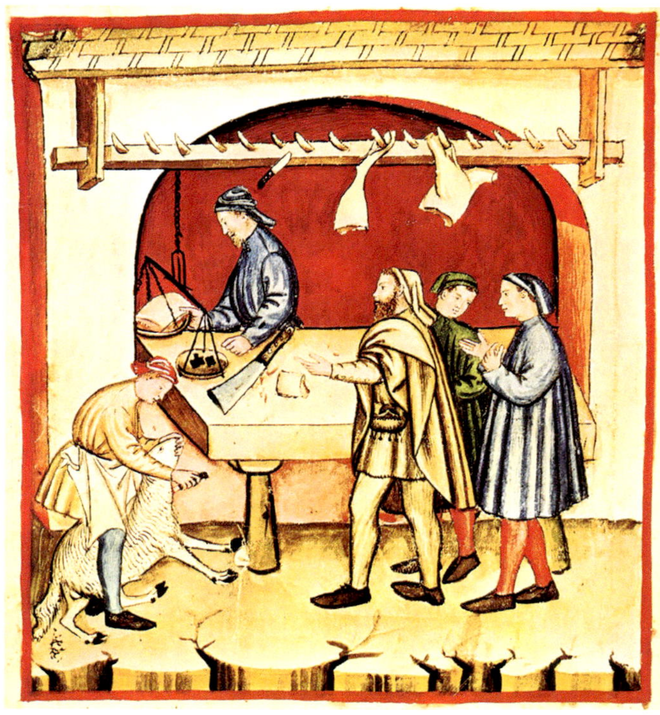

A butcher performing his trade in a traditional manner. (From *Tacuinum Sanitatis, Casanatense,* fourteenth century)

Fasting, in terms of just abstaining from meat, was also strictly observed during the Tudor period. On Wednesdays, Fridays and Saturdays it was acceptable to eat fish, game and poultry. Often dairy and eggs were also forbidden. Later in the medieval period almonds provided a good substitute for dairy. For people on the coast, year-round fresh fish wasn't a problem; if you lived inland, you'd struggle with salted herring or cod. Monks ate mammals and sea birds, like puffins, justifying them as beasts that ate fish, therefore were more fishlike and suitable fodder for fast days. There are some medieval accounts of winters being fuelled by alcohol to make up for restricted diets.

Pie making is most often associated with this period, although its origins are much earlier. Traditionally meat and fish was encased in a sturdy salt dough which protected the flesh in cooking and sealed in all the meat juices. The pastry casing and crust, known by the medieval period as 'coffins', was simply discarded. Pies also served as a method of preservation. A small hole was cut into the top and filled with hot fat, a similar technique to that of making confits. To *confit* is a French term applied to the cooking of meat in a heavy grease or oil, something that was also done in the medieval period, leaving it to cool in the fat before sealing it in that same fat to prevent it spoiling. In the Middle Ages the word was also associated with fruits, nuts and seeds, particularly aniseeds, that were coated in a hot syrup, often with spices, before being dried and stored. It seems the words confit and comfit were interchangeable until the later 1700s, when a comfit was only applied to sweetmeats.

The following pie recipe is taken from Harleian Manuscript number 4016, possibly dating to around 1450 and collated with other recipes as part of Thomas Austin's *Two Fifteenth Century Cook Books.*

An abbey cellarer testing his wine. (Illumination from a copy of *Li livres dou Santé*, British Library, Sloane 2435, f. 44v)

Pastry cases were called 'coffins' in the medieval period. (© Emma Kay)

Pies of Parys (Paris)

Take and smyte faire buttes of pork and buttes of vele togidre, and put hit in a faire potte. And putte thereto faire broth and a quantite of wyne, and lete all boile togidre til hit be ynogh; and þen take hit fro the fire and lete kele a litel, and cast therto raw yolkes of eyren and pudre of gyngevere, sugre and salt, and minced dates, reysyns of corence. Make then coffyns of feyre past, and do it therynne, and kerve it and lete bake ynogh.[12]

Pastry tarts were as popular as pies and made good fish dishes, particularly for fasting days, like this recipe for Lent found in the Arundel Manuscripts, which includes both fourteenth- and fifteenth-century references, as well as the *Forme of Cury*. It's also a recipe that exemplifies the medieval trend for pairing meat and fish with fruit – undoubtedly another Middle Eastern influence. Note that there were open tarts and covered tarts. What exactly made a covered tart a tart and not a pie, other than that they weren't raised, is difficult to determine, although tarts containing more liquid (in particular almond milk) appear to be left open. Later in the seventeenth century tart fillings combined eggs and milk to make more of a quiche or, as it was known then in Britain, a French tart. Similalrly, *Flaumpeyns* were a type of shallow pork and cheese tart or pie popular from around the 1300s until at least the fifteenth century.

Tart for Lenton

Take figges and raisfinges, and wash hom in wyne, and grinde hom, and appuls and peres clene pared, and the corke tane out [the cores taken out]; then take fresh famon, or codlynge, or hadok, and grinde hit, and medel [mix] hit al togedur, and do hit in a coffin, and do therto pouder of ginger, and of canelle [cinnamon] ande clowes, [cloves] and maces; and plaunte hit above [decorate it on top] with pynes,[peppercorns] or almonds, and prunes, and dates quartert, then cover thi coffin, and bake hit, and ferve hit forthe.[13]

The following is my modified recipe, which I have not enclosed in pastry. If you really want to make an authentic yet contemporary medieval dish, then this has many of the components and flavours of that age, even if it does at first feel a little alien.

Medieval Fish Tart
85 g dried figs
20 g raisins
1 small apple cored and chopped small
150 g salmon, cod or haddock
100 ml milk
2 eggs beaten
½ tsp each of ground ginger, cinnamon, cloves, mace and black peppercorns
Blanched almonds
Dried prunes
Dried dates stoned and halved

- Start by making your own pastry by mixing 160 g flour and 80 g butter with a few tablespoons of water and then leaving it to chill for an hour or so in the fridge, or use a packet of ready roll.
- Soak figs and raisins in enough red wine to cover for a couple of hours, chop small and mix with the apple.
- Heat the oven to 200°C/180°C fan/gas 6.
- Roll out or just push the pastry into a 20 cm diameter greased flan case. Prick the surface with a fork all over. Line with baking paper and cover with baking beans. Bake for 15 minutes.
- In a pan poach the fish in the milk for around 4 minutes. Do not discard the milk.
- Remove the baking beans and baking paper and cook the pastry for a further 15 minutes. Set aside and let it cool.
- Lightly break the fish into small chunks or flakes and mix together with the milk, beaten eggs, figs, raisins, and apple. Add the ginger, cinnamon, cloves, mace and crushed black peppercorns and season with salt to taste, to the mixture and use your hands to work it altogether before adding it to the tart case.

Reworking of a medieval fish tart for Lent. (© Emma Kay)

- Top with the almonds, prunes, and dates.
- Return to the oven and cook for about 25 minutes. Leave to cool for a couple of minutes before serving as you would a quiche.

The French word *farce*, often translated as 'farts', refers to what we understand better as forcemeat, used as a stuffing or standalone dish of finely chopped and seasoned meat or fish was also popular during this part of the medieval era. The word also took a confusing turn as a pastry-related dainty dough ball, which could be sweet or savoury.

Sauces

Early Medieval

Vinegar is the by-product of any carbohydrate source that has been left to rot and ferment, a process where the natural sugars or starches in organic matter get converted into acidic gases or liquids. So, in theory you can create a vinegar from grapes, wine, berries, honey, grains, beets, whey from milk and so on. Early communities were quick to adopt fermentation in this way and vinegar was used to preserve all manner of foodstuffs. Early Egyptian and Middle Eastern communities were producing vinegars from dates and palm, so it's likely Europeans were too. There are many Old English vinegar-related, or *eced*, words, including a wine vinegar *eced-win*, which would have been stored in *eced-fœts* or vinegar vats.[14] The world's earliest evidence of fermentation was discovered in Sweden and consisted of fermented fish that was 9,200 years old. The ancient site of Sunnansund was carefully excavated using fine-mesh sieves, revealing vast areas of densely packed fish bones. As people didn't have access to salt, they acidified the fish using things like pine bark and seal fat, then wrapped it all up in seal and wild boar skins before burying it in a muddy pit. You need a cold climate for this type of fermentation, so it's not out of the question to consider that Vikings in Britian did the same thing.

It's not difficult to imagine how a practical liquid like vinegar didn't take long to become something that was also used as a sauce. Undoubtedly, if you preserved and stored raw goods in vinegar it would be just as easy to tip the entire contents out and cook it in its vinegary liquid when the time came. So, it's probably safe to say that both water that was flavoured with meat and vegetables as a broth and vinegar would have been the earliest known sauces to accompany meat, fish, vegetables, eggs and, well, anything really.

Vinegar is referenced frequently throughout the old leechdoms to accompany all manner of remedies from sore gums and tapeworms to headaches. For a saucier culinary reference of this generation, we might look to Middle Eastern trends and their passion for mustard sauce.

Mustard sauce

Pick over and sift through mustard seeds to get rid of dust, twigs, rotten seeds, and other impurities that might be in it. Pound the seeds thoroughly. If this proves to be difficult, add to the seeds a piece of cotton. This will make pounding them much easier. Once you finish pounding, add to the seeds an equal amount of walnuts, and continue pounding. Then pour as much as you like of vinegar and strain the mixture

> in a fine sieve. You will get fine mustard that is whiter than sea foam itself (*zabad*). Take the foam only, and add to it a little salt and serve it, God willing.
>
> Make sauce with the remaining mix [by adding] pounded raisins and vinegar. It will be fabulous indeed.[15]

Interestingly, the old Anglo-Saxon leeches reference both mustard and peppercorns as ingredients used to flavour dishes, and there is archaeological evidence of their presence in the British Isles at this time. There's nothing to say that both of these ingredients weren't crushed down and mixed with a vinegar, honey or broth of some sort to make crude sauces from the juices of the fish or meat as it cooked, just as they were simultaneously in other parts of the world.

I like to think that this very simple sauce from *Apicius*, which arguably could date anywhere from the first to the fifth centuries, was also one that was inherited by the Anglo-Saxons in post-Roman-occupied England to accompany widely eaten fish dishes. At this stage I feel it is important to mention that many old manuscripts have over the years been translated and reinterpreted by different scholars. Most of the references in this book refer to the 1936 translation of *Apicius* compiled by J. Vehling. It has been considered that other translations, most notably that of Barbara Flower and Elisabeth Rosenbaum, are more authentic. I will leave this question hovering in the air for readers to make up their own minds.

Reworking of mustard sauce showing the 'foam'. (© Emma Kay)

Mustard seeds and peppercorns. (© Emma Kay)

Prepare the fish carefully; in the mortar put salt, coriander seed, crush and mix well; turn the fish therein, put it in a pan, cover it and seal it with plaster, cook it in the oven. When done retire the fish from the pan sprinkle with strong vinegar and serve.[16]

Eleventh to Thirteenth Centuries

Scholars Faith Wallis and Giles Gasper's discovery several years ago of a series of recipes originally confined to Durham Cathedral Priory offer insight into twelfth-century sauce making in England. Roman *Salsamentum* were originally salty liquids associated with food preservation. By the 1100s these had evolved into sauces used for a variety of purposes, including garnishing and basting. Here are a few of the translated sauce recipes discovered in Durham:

Acetum confortat appetitum. Accipe salviam petroselinum piper mentam et contere et distempera cum aceto tale salsamentum dicitur pictamentum.

Vinegar strengthens the appetite. Take sage, parsley, pepper, and mint; grind them and mix with vinegar. This is called Poitou sauce.

Petrosilini et saluie succum cum aceto distemperatum cum pipere et allio fortiter trito commisce. et cum his carnem sulcitam comede.

Mix juice of parsley and sage which has been mixed with vinegar with finely ground pepper and garlic, and eat sausage with this.[17]

Vinegar remained at the heart of all medieval sauce making. Small crab apples were sour and used to make verjuice, a type of vinegar for sauce making. This could be kept for around a year. Verjuice/verjus has a complex legacy that extends to very early communities and became extremely popular in recipes of the later medieval period. As well as crab apples it was typically made from sorrel or unripe grapes. Verjuice appears with regularity across medieval culinary manuscripts from Italy, Spain, England, Germany, France and Holland.

The following example is from a translation of the culinary treatise *Le Menagier* compiled by the 'Goodman of Paris' for his young wife in France in 1393.

Sorrel Verjuice

Bray [grind] sorrel very well without the stems and dilute it with old white verjuice and do not strain the sorrel, but bray it well. or thus: bray parsley and sorrel or blades of corn. Item, vine buds, that is those that are young and tender, without stems.[18]

Recreation of Poitou sauce with home-made vinegar. (© Emma Kay)

Le Viandier, a French recipe collection copied several times during the Middle Ages, the earliest version boasting a provenance of around 1300, goes into great detail about which sauces should be paired with which meats. While a parsley sauce was thought to bring out the best of the snout, feet and ears of a pig, its intestines were more suited apparently to a garlic sauce or verjuice. Roe deer meat required a hot pepper sauce or a sauce of garlic, cinnamon, ginger and almond milk if served in the winter. Fish was best paired with mostly green sauces made with sage, parsley and spices.[19]

Food preservation was central to early medieval society and the following sauce from Henrik Harpestaeng's thirteenth-century Danish recipe compilation also acted as a preserving agent for game meats.

Game in men's sauce

Quomodo condiantur assature in salso supradicto. (Q5) Thawær man wil af hennæ hauæ. tha must one wællæ hennæ wæl .i. a pannæ ofnæ hetæ gløthær utæn brandæ. and one must take brathæ of hiort ællær ra. well lard and roast them well. oc skæræ them well brethæ. oc thæn timæ thæn salsæ ær kald tha shall wildbrath .i. lay geese méth littæt salt oc tæt ma lyggæ thre ukæ. Swa mughæ man haldæ goth hiortæ brath. geese and ducks. of man cut them thiokkæ. Thættæ ær the bæstæ salsæ thær hærrémæn hauæ.

How to cook dishes in the aforementioned gravy (men's gravy). If you want it, you have to pour it (sauce) into a pan on top of (on) hot embers without burning. And you have to take roast venison or well-fatted venison and fry it well. And cut that brad well. And when the sauce is cold, the wild boar must be put in with a little salt and it (all) must lie for three weeks. This is how you can keep good venison, geese and duck if you cut them thickly. It's the best gravy that gentlemen have.[20]

Le Viandier de Taillevent, from a fifteenth-century edition.

Late Medieval

Just as vinegar sustained people the centuries before, by the fourteenth century it was considered integral to the 'curing' of the plague. As such, vinegar would have been used extensively during the Black Death, as an accompaniment to meals, when mixed with sugar and spices or even sprinkled around the house together with rose water, on hands and faces. It was even added to bread mixtures.

It's worth mentioning here that *theriac* or, as the English christened it, Venice treacle, made from a vast array of fermented herbs, roots, fruits, flowers and leaves, oils, gums and animal parts, also became a hugely popular 'antidote' for the Black Death in England.

By the fifteenth century the French word 'sauce', taken from the Latin *salsa* had become established in culinary texts. Thomas Dawson's 1596 *The Good Huswifes Jewell* references many sauces: sweet-based fruit sauces with barberries, mustard sauces for fish and this onion sauce to accompany rabbit:

> **A sauce for a Conie**
> Cut Onions in rundels [circles] and frie them in butter, then put to them wine Vine-ger, salt, ginger, camomill and pepper, and a litle suger, and let it boyle till it be good and fast, then serue it vpon the conie.[21]

Prolific sauce references earlier in this era can also be found in scholar and Oxford English Dictionary contributor Thomas Austin's translations of Harleian manuscripts (assembled by Robert Harley) 279 and 4016, *c.* 1430 and 1450 respectively.

Consuming theriac. (From the twelfth-century *Livre de la Thériaque de Paris*)

The flour, fat and milk combination sauces better known as a roux are given a much later provenance, although a flour-and-milk-based sauce called *sermstele* seasoned with garlic, salt and pepper is included in Austin's compilation of fifteenth-century recipes and reminiscent of its evolution.

Sauce sermstele. (Yellow Garlic Sauce)
Take Milke and a litul floure, And caste hit in a potte, And lete boile al togidur al thyn; and whan hit is wel boyled, take and stampe garlek small, and caste there-to pouder of peper, and salt, And then serue hit forth.[22]

White sauces were also prepared by mixing liquids with finely ground almonds at this time, which began substituting the age-old use of bread as a thickener.

Just as garum was the fishy ketchup of the Romans, Cameline sauce was a medieval classic and appears in numerous texts. My favourite example is the one published in *Liber Cure Cocorum*, a culinary manuscript written partly in comical verse and often attributed to Lancashire, dating to *c.* 1430. There were many versions, all served with a variety of meats, with cinnamon being a common factor.

Sauce Cameline
Take dried currants and small kernels
Of nuts, and take away the shells,
Take crust of bread and cloves together,
And powder made of good ginger,

Recreation of sauce sermstele. (© Emma Kay)

> Flour of cinnamon you shall take, then
> Pound all together, as I teach you,
> In a mortar and salt thereto;
> Mix all with vinegar, then have you done,
> And serve it forth; this is fine sauce,
> That men call *cameline*.[23]

Another definitive sauce of the Middle Ages was Galyntyne or Galantine, a very thick sauce consisting of grated bread, broth, wine and spices, sometimes using the South Asian spice galingale/galangal. It is referenced frequently in the fourteenth-century English cookery compilation *The Forme of Cury*. John Russell suggests cooking lampreys in a pie, removing them and placing them on thin slices of bread before pouring over the galentyne, adding cinnamon and red wine, and mincing the lampreys prior to serving it all in the sauce on a hot plate.

3

Dairy, Eggs, Fruit and Veg

Dairy and Eggs

Early Medieval

While we take for granted the availability of year-round eggs today, hens naturally only lay eggs during the spring and summer months. As such, eggs would once have been pickled in brine and vinegar and kept for up to four months.

The sixth-century *De Obseruatione Ciborum* (On the Observance of Foods), written by a physian called Anthimus, is thought to be the first cookery book to come out of those provinces considered to be French or Frankish with Latin and Mediterranean influences. The following recipe for chicken in egg whites is similar to one found in the Roman cookbook *De Re Coquinaria*, credited to Caelius Apicius and written around the same time. It's likely the contents of both manuscripts would have permeated into other European regions, particularly those with Roman and Frankish connections.

> **Afrutum and eggs**
>
> Greek *afrutum*, which in Latin is called *spumeum* ['foaming'], is made of chicken and egg white. But put in a great deal of egg white, so that it becomes like foam - the dish *afrutem* – ; thus pour over it prepared gravy and *oenogarum* (a Roman fish sauce also known as garum) in a bowl mixing it so that it makes a little mound. And place the bowl on the coals so that the liquids steam and cook the *afrutem*. And put this bowl in the middle of a platter and spread over it some unmixed wine and honey, and eat it with a spoon or a tender new growth.[1]

I imagine this is similar to an egg white frittata with chicken and slightly fishy undertones.

Combinations of eggs with vegetables, herbs (known as *wortes* in the Middle Ages), meats with or without broth brought together as a solid mass like an omelette or scrambled and served with or without sauces were very popular during the early medieval period. Perhaps this was indeed a forerunner of the French omelette.

In Norse mythology the sacred goat Heidrun was worshipped as an animal that discharged mead from her teats.[2] Throughout the earlier medieval era, goats' milk, cheese and butter was highly prized, a welcome addition at feasts and for the average family diet. Theologian and twelfth-century writer Alexander Neckam of St Albans noted in his book *De Naturis Rerum* (On the Book of Things) that: 'The milk of the she-goat was efficacious against many diseases; and the flesh of the kid was a delicious as well as a very wholesome food.'[3]

However, after the eleventh century a range of archival records dictate that the goat was fairly rare livestock in the British Isles, confined only in small numbers to the west and north of England.[4]

In later medieval culinary texts, goats are generally only referenced as young kids culled for roasting and not exploited for their milk. However, as little evidence exists of poorer communities and what they were eating at this time, we shouldn't discount the possibility that small farmsteads may indeed have kept goats for milk and cheese consumption.

Sheep's milk was also an essential element of the early medieval diet. England had a thriving wool trade, exporting to Frankish and Scandinavian regions and cheesemaking largely revolved around the milk they capitalised on from their herds. Cows were predominantly working creatures, so it fell to sheep to provide the bulk of the dairy products.

Another important factor to include when considering the consumption of dairy in the past was the inherent intolerance for lactose across many communities. This took hundreds of years to genetically alter, as societies steadily integrated and altered as a consequence of immigration in the British Isles. It probably remained commonplace to continue making butter, cheese and milk from sheep and goats for quite some time. The Romans undoubtedly improved cheesemaking in England, in terms of variety and

The sacred goat Heidrun from an Icelandic manuscript.

Separation of Sheep and Goats. (Byzantine Metropolitan Museum of Art)

Preparing and serving cheese. (From *Tacuinum Sanitatis*, fourteenth century)

how it could be used as a diverse ingredient. There were cheese-cakes (literally rounds of sweetened cheese), cheese in soups and stews and gratins or even jellies, like this interesting recipe which requires chilling in the snow taken from the assumed fifth-century culinary manuscript *De Re Coquinaria,* better known as *Apicius.*

Apician Jelly (Salacattabia Apiciana)

Put in the mortar celery seed, dry pennyroyal, dry mint, ginger, fresh coriander, seedless raisins, honey, vinegar, oil and wine; crush it together in order to make a dressing of it. Now Place 3 pieces of Picentian bread in a mould, interlined with pieces of cooked chicken, cooked sweetbreads of calf or lamb, cheese, pignolia nuts, cucumbers [pickles], finely chopped dry onions [shallots] covering the whole with jellified broth. Bury the mould in snow up to the rim; unmould, sprinkle with the above dressing and serve.[5]

One other interesting fact when considering the early history of dairy can be found in the Icelandic saga *Sturlunga.* Written in the twelfth/thirteenth centuries by various authors but covering Scandinavian history from the 1100s, it recalls a story in which the main protagonist Gizurr remains hidden from his would-be assassins in a vat of Skyr and survives. The thick, popular commercial yoghurt of the same name today was being made by Vikings over a thousand years ago. Vats containing archaeological remains of Skyr have been discovered in Scandinavia, where it would originally have been made from sour milk, mixed with rennet and made into a soft cheese.

Eleventh to Thirteenth Centuries

According to the poem 'Regimen Sanitatis Salernitanum' (the health and diet regime) dated anywhere between the eleventh and thirteenth centuries in Salerno, milk and cheese were considered melancholic and harmful to sick people, nor was it helpful to those with a fever or general aches and pains. This well-received verse published by a renowned medical school also advocated the consumption of goat's and camel milk for killer diseases, while praising ass's milk as the most nutritious and butter as a useful laxative.[6]

Primitive cheese press. (© Emma Kay)

Plunger churn, the style of which remains ancient in design. (© Emma Kay)

The most coveted milk of all throughout the medieval period was almond milk. It is a staple of just about every culinary text in Europe and even appears in the compilation of northern European recipes, largely from Denmark and Germany, contained in *Libellus De Arte Coquinaria* (*The Little Book of Culinary Arts*) with a provenance of the early thirteenth century.[7] Part of this compilation includes extracts from Danish medic Henrik Harpestaeng, who died in 1244 and whose writings were influenced by his widespread travels overseas. Henrik's recipes are heavily almond based, with titles like 'How is almond butter made' and 'How is sour milk made from almonds'. They are indicative of the way in which non-native recipes were universally transposed throughout the Middle Ages.

Almond butter
Quomodo fit butirum de amygdalis (Q3) One must takæ ammandæl's kiærnæ and make of milk and latæ for watn. oc latæ .i. a grutæ oc gøræ thæt warm .a. gloat. oc latæ to saffron well writhet. and salt. oc édyk to matæ oc make dense hot everything to dense thiuknær. Thæn timæ hæt ær yuært thiukt. latæ dense .i. et klæthe syth samæn sum posæ oc hængæ tight .a. a weg all to watlæn er of ill. oc take sithen thick ut oc make of smørslagh.

How to make butter from almonds:
You have to take almond kernels and make almond milk from them and add water. And put them in a pot and heat it over embers, and add grated saffron, and salt and vinegar to taste and heat it all until it thickens. When it (mass) is thick, pour it into a cloth sewn together as a bag and hang it against a wall until the moisture has drained off. And then take it (mass) out and make butter from it.

You can make your own almond butter simply by roasting about 450 g of whole raw almonds at 180°C, 350°F for about 10 minutes. Cool for another 5–10 minutes, then simply blitz them in a food processor until you get crumbs, then a ball and finally creamy almond butter.

You can even omit roasting the almonds and just go straight to the food processor stage, but this will take about 15 minutes of pounding before you achieve your butter. Serve on wholemeal toast or rice cakes for a really healthy snack.

Sour Milk from Almonds

Quomodo fit lac acetuosum de amygdalis
After eating, one must takæ ammandæls kiærnæ oc make thær of thiuk milk oc latæ thær to edikæ ællær win oc sætae .a. hot hot hot hot hot hot hot hot hot everything to close thiuknær. thæt ær æm got sum suur faræ milk.

How to make sour milk from almonds:
Then you have to take almond kernels and make thick milk from them and add vinegar or wine to it and put it all on hot coals until it thickens. It is as good as sour sheep's milk.[8]

Eggs were repeatedly integrated into medicinal remedies before and during the twelfth and thirteenth centuries. The old Anglo-Saxon leeches contain numerous references, including the application of egg whites for broken limbs, which may have been related to the binding properties of hardened whites. In Giles Gasper and Faith Wallis's research of the manuscripts belonging to twelfth-century Durham Cathedral, they unearthed a treatment for indigestion involving hard-boiled eggs, quartered and stirred into a mint and vinegar sauce. I remain sceptical of this one, knowing as I do how high the acidic content of eggs is.[9]

Fresh almond butter. (© Emma Kay)

Late Medieval

Towards the end of the medieval era new methods of getting creative with cheese were being adopted, such as this possible first ever recipe for cheese straws in *Le Menagier de Paris* which are absolutely delicious.

Pipefarces

Take egg yolks and flour and salt, and a little wine, and beat together strongly, and cheese chopped in thin slices, and then roll the slices of cheese in the batter, and then fry in an iron skillet with oil in it. This can also be made using beef marrow.[10]

English manuscript Douce 257, named after Francis Douce circa 1381, which is housed in the Bodleian Library, provides an excellent early example of how milk and eggs were frequently combined to make all manner of dishes.

The curiously named Blank Desure/Blank Desyre/Blonk Desore (desire possibly being a derivative of Syria) was clearly a popular dish considering the many variations that were published across numerous texts throughout the Middle Ages. Some researchers confuse these recipes with blancmange, but I think it was more like a Middle Eastern-inspired rice pudding. Note that this is a smooth rice pudding with rice flour, which was known in the Middle East as Bahatta or Muhallabiyya.[11]

Blank desure

Tak þe olkys of egges sodyn & temper it wyþ mylk of a kow. & do þerto comyn & safroun & flowre of ris or wastel bred myed, & grynd in a morter & temper it vp wyþ þe milk; & mak it boyle & do þerto wit of egges coruyn smal. & tak fat chese & kerf þerto wan þe licour is boylyd, & serue it forþ.[12]

Recreation of fourteenth-century pipefarces, or medieval cheese straws. (© Emma Kay)

White Syrian pudding (my own translation)

Take the yolks of eggs, soak and mix them with cow's milk and cumin and saffron and rice flour, or wastel breadcrumbs mixed with milk. Boil it with eggs (hard-boiled and chopped small) and take some full fat cheese and cut this thereto when the liquor is boiled and serve.

The same technique for separating the yolks and boiling the whites of eggs in recipes around this time can be found throughout Europe. Whether this method itself originated in the Middle East or not is debatable, but it's interesting that we have lost this way of preparing eggs in modern cooking – in England anyway.

Towards the latter part of the medieval period it became typical to cook a lot of foods in butter, opposed to oil or broths, and it was used routinely in numerous dishes to fry, thicken and add flavour – undoubtedly an influence of French cuisine.

A Book of Cookrye by someone simply signed 'A.W.' that was put together in 1591 includes a sophisticated recipe for buttered loaf, which is very similar to a brioche with spices.

A Buttered Loafe

Take very fine flowre and yolks of Egs, sweet butter, yest, cloves, mace, sugar, sinamon, ginger, and woork it togither and make them in little loves, and when they are baked inough, set a good deale of sweet butter upon a chafingdish and coles, then cut your loaf in three peeces and butter it, then strew sugar betwixt every peece and serve it out.[13]

The ingredient 'sweet butter' is also mentioned some eight times in Thomas Dawson's *The Good Huswifes Jewell* (1596) and crops up a staggering twenty-six times in the recipes within John Murrell's *A New Booke of Cookerie* from 1615. This, surprisingly, is not a reference to butter sweetened with sugar or other natural sweeteners. According to a 1799 edition of *Annals of Agriculture*, sweet butter was simply a term for good-quality butter made using utensils that were exceptionally clean. It required frequent stirring and for all of the residual buttermilk to be drained and removed.[14]

There's one early French toast/eggy bread recipe essential to this period called Pain Perdu/Payn purdeuz/puredew, which was allegedly a French creation, although given that most French recipes often lead back to the Middle East I remain sceptical, particularly as early Arabic cooking was heavily influenced by egg and bread combinations. There was also a village near the coastal town of Atlit in Israel, now long forgotten but once a Crusader stronghold called Pain Perdu, which I can't help thinking may have a strong connection to this dish.[15]

The following is my own reworking of a fifteenth-century recipe. Instead of soaking the bread in egg and lard, I've substituted the lard for butter.

Pain Perdu

- Take two slices of white bread and toast them.
- Soak the slices of toast in a mix of 3 beaten eggs and 40 g of melted butter, seasoned with salt and pepper.
- Once fully coated, fry in butter or vegetable oil until crispy.[16]

Churned milk to make butter. (© Emma Kay)

The Crusader fortress of Athlit, Israel, 21 March 2007. (אסף.צ, משתמש:אסף.צ נוצר על ידי, CC BY-SA 3.0)

Pain perdu (French toast). (© Emma Kay)

Fruit and Veg

Early Medieval

I think there was a lot of superstition and fear around mushrooms in the medieval period. They certainly are not cited in any detail within the old leechdoms, other than one reference as a remedy for glandular swellings behind the ear. The Old English word for an edible mushroom was *meteswamm*, so they were possibly eaten as foraging food or as emergency food in times of hardship. There is also a real lack of recorded recipes containing mushrooms throughout the whole medieval period other than in Italian, some French and overwhelmingly in Hungarian medieval culinary texts. In fact, vegetables generally do not tend to be listed specifically, other than in monastery garden lists and in herbal remedies throughout the Middle Ages. This may have something to do with the fact that they were commonplace and referencing them was irrelevant; it was a given that they would be there as salads (often served warm) and side dishes to accompany meat-heavy meals.

Poorer communities would unquestionably have found vegetables invaluable. The Romans gifted the British Isles with a range of new fruit and vegetables, over 50 new plant foods in total from onions to lentils, fennel and radishes, cherries and pears, walnuts, damsons, celery and exotic spices and herbs.

Leeks were a staple vegetable of the Anglo-Saxon era. They are mentioned regularly across the old leechdoms and were venerated in Scandinavian folklore. Prior to the Romans, however, the British Isles would have survived on a limited diet of beet-type root vegetables, sorrel, tansy and beans and peas by the Bronze Age, along with seaweeds and other edible leafy plants like fat hen and docks. Crab apples, hawthorn, sloes, bilberries and rowan berries are all also native to the British Isles. Following Roman occupation and a thriving economy in trade, England benefitted from a luscious variety of apples, plums (often dried as prunes) strawberries, raspberries, elderberries, medlars, etc., which

Fresco of Adam and Eve in the Garden of Eden, flanking a giant psychoactive Amanita muscaria mushroom and a cluster of four mushrooms at the base. The serpent offers Eve the fruit from the Tree of the Knowledge of Good and Evil. (Courtesy of Aranthama, CC BY-SA 4.0)

Fennel soaking. (© Emma Kay)

Freshly picked sloe berries. (© Emma Kay)

continued either to be cultivated or imported. There is even an archaeological argument for the presence of figs, and of course grapes, for winemaking. Garlic also featured on the menu in the early medieval period – the bulb variety as well as native wild garlic, along with a host of spices that are often mistakenly attributed to the later medieval period. Wealthier Anglo-Saxons imported pepper, ginger and cinnamon among other luxury items into England to enhance a variety of dishes.[17]

It is important to reiterate that herbs were considered edible vegetables and their application to a variety of dishes and drinks during the early medieval period are integral to a much wider narrative around the medicinal, ritual and spiritual properties they were known for. Cumin, parsley and peppercorns for the bowels; fennel, rose and rue for cloudy eyes; coriander mixed with breast milk and honey for sore ears; mint for intestinal worms; and henbane for toothache.[18] The list is endless and fluctuated widely as the medieval period progressed.

Eleventh to Thirteenth Centuries

Alexander Neckam advised that all manor house gardens of the time he was living, which was the twelfth century, should yield the following produce: parsley, cost (costmary) fennel, southernwood, coriander, sage, savory, hyssop, mint, rue, dittany, smallage, pellitory, lettuce,

Raisins and figs in wine.
(© Emma Kay)

Fourteenth-century dentist, complete with silver forceps and a necklace of large teeth, extracting the tooth of a seated man. (British Library)

Ladies in a garden embroidering, 1600s. (British Library)

garden cress, and pionies, onions, leeks, garlic, pumpkins and shallots. The cucumber, the poppy, the daffodil and brank-ursine (acantus).

There should also be pottage herbs such as beets, herb mercury, orach, sorrel and mallows. Anise, mustard, white pepper, absinthe or horehound. Neckam goes on to say that medlars, quinces, pears, peaches, pomegranates, citrus fruits, almonds, dates and figs are also all essential.[19]

Obviously, if you were poor a fancy garden like this with round-the-clock access to fresh fruit and vegetables wasn't likely. Greens boiled in bone marrow or leftovers from the philanthropic monastic tables of the era was most of what you could hope for. Windfallen and hedgerow fruit may also have been your only option if you weren't wealthy.

Commercial relations amid Spanish provinces and England between 1200 and 1500 were very active and, as such, a shared understanding of one another's cultures would inevitably have involved an exchange of food and drink. Aubergines were not recognised in the British Isles until at least the sixteenth century, and realistically were not eaten with any regularity until the twentieth century. Nonetheless, this is a dish inspired by the Muslim-occupied regions of Europe and it was possibly widely replicated or modified.

The *gourds* mentioned in this thirteenth-century recipe, which has all the hallmarks of a giant vegetable omelette, refers to squash, which appear in some English culinary medieval recipes and may have been available via the Americas much earlier than their commonly reputed European provenance of the sixteenth century.

Black pears. (© Emma Kay)

Map of Spain and Portugal in the 1500s.

Gourd harvest. (From *Tacuinum Sanitatis* of Vienna, fourteenth century)

Jannâniyya (the Gardener's Dish).

It was the custom among us to make this in the flower and vegetable gardens. If you make it in summer or fall, take saltwort, Swiss chard, gourd, small eggplants, 'eyes' of fennel, fox-grapes, the best parts of tender gourd and flesh of ribbed cucumber and smooth cucumber; chop all this very small, as vegetables are chopped, and cook with water and salt; then drain off the water. Take a clean pot and in it pour a little water and a lot of oil, pounded onion, garlic, pepper, coriander seed and caraway; put on a moderate fire and when it has boiled, put in the boiled vegetables. When it has finished cooking, add grated or pounded bread and dissolved [sour] dough, and break over it as many eggs as you are able, and squeeze in the juice of tender coriander and of mint, and leave on the hearthstone until the eggs set. If you make it in spring, then [use] lettuce, fennel, peeled fresh fava beans, spinach, Swiss chard, carrots, fresh cilantro and so on, cook it all and add the spices already indicated, plenty of oil, cheese, dissolved [sour] dough and eggs.[20]

Late Medieval

Potatoes would have first arrived in the British Isles sometime during the end of the medieval era, but they were treated with dubiety and not widely adopted in cooking until several centuries later. One of the first cookery writers to include potato recipes was John Murrell in his *A New Booke of Cookerie*, published in 1615. The marrow here is not the vegetable variety, which didn't exist in England until the 1800s, rather it refers to marrowbone, a common and popular ingredient of the Middle Ages.

A Marrow toast

MJnce colde parboyld Ueale, and
Suit very fine, and sweet Hearbs
each by themselues, and then mingle
them together with Sugar, Nutmeg,
Sinamon, Rosewater, grated bread,
the yolkes of two or three new layd
Egges: open the minst meat, and
couer it with the marrow. Then put
your toast into the Pipkin with the
vppermost of some strong broth: let
it boyle with large Mace, a Fagot of
sweet hearbs, scum them passing cleane,
and let them boyle almost drye. Then
take Potato-rootes boyld, or Chest-nuts,
Skirrootes, or Almonds, boyled
in white Wine, and for want of Wine
you may take Uergis and Sugar.[21]

Tomatoes were also introduced at this time via the South American territories and grown in some of the bigger gardens of the nobility, but like potatoes they weren't commercially cultivated until around the 1800s and don't appear in any medieval culinary recipes.

As previously mentioned, fast days, also known as ember days, were integral to society. This is where vegetables came into their own and would have been used creatively in recipes such as this ember day tart from the *Forme of Cury*.

> **TART IN YMBRE (Ember)**
> Take and parboile Oynouns presse out þe water & hewe hem smale. take brede & bray it in a morter. and temper it up with Ayren. do þerto butter, safroun and salt. & raisouns corauns. & a litel sugur with powdour douce. and bake it in a trape. & serue it forth.[22]

Crustardes were open or sometimes closed tarts, an ancestor of the quiche, filled with beaten egg and milk/broth combinations of fish, meat, vegetables, nuts and so on. The 1390 edition of the *Forme of Cury* is laden with crustarde recipes and you can find an example in Chapter 2.

William Langland's fourteenth-century text *Piers Ploughman* provides us with a little insight into what poorer communities may have eaten towards the latter part of the Middle Ages. 'Hunger' is a symbolic figure designed to instil pressure on Piers for him and his colleagues to work harder, grow more crops and remain sustained throughout the farming year. The following dialogue is between Piers and 'Hunger' describing what the industrious ploughman has to eat. Meat was clearly a luxury that he does not have. Curds (cruddes) and oatcakes (haver-cake), loaves of bread made with beans and bran for his children, parsley, a thick meatless soup (porettes) and cabbages and livestock to work his plough is all Piers has to see him through until Lammas (the harvest), although it is unclear exactly what period of time that is.

> I have no penny, quod Piers, pullets for to buy,
> Ne neither geese nor pigs, but two green cheeses,
> A few cruddes and cream, and a haver-cake,
> And two loaves of beans and bran ybake for my fauntis.
> And yet I say, by my soul, I have no salt bacon,
> Nor no cookeney, by Christ, collops for to maken.
> And I have percil and porettes and many kole-plantes,
> And eke a cow and a claf, and a cart-mare
> To draw afield my dung the while the draught lasteth.[23]

Contemporary quiche.

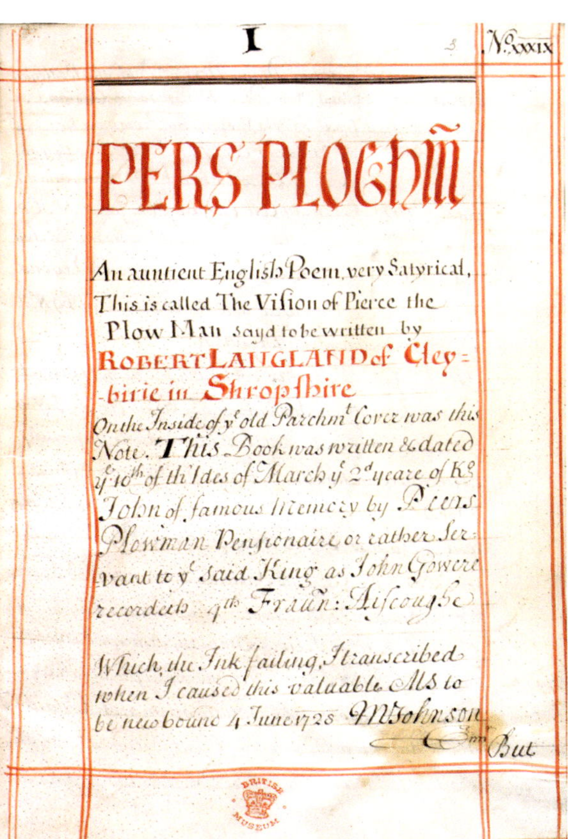

I N.o XXXIX

PERS PLOGHM

An auntient English Poem, very Satyrical,
This is called The Vision of Pierce the
Plow Man sayd to be written by
ROBERT LANGLAND of Cley-
-birie in Shropshire
On the Inside of ye old Parchmt Cover was this
Note. This Book was written & dated
ye 10th of th' Ides of March ye 2d yeare of Kg
John of famous Memory by Piers
Plowman Pensionaire or rather Ser-
vant to ye said King as John Gowere
recordeth 9th Fraun: Aiscoughe

Which, the Ink failing, I transcribed
when I caused this valuable MS to
be new bound 4 June 1728 M Johnson
But

Piers Plowman by William Langland (C version), late fourteenth century. (MS 35157, British Library)

Workers threshing and pig feeding from a book of hours from the Workshop of the Master of James IV of Scotland. (Flemish, *c.* 1541)

4

Sweet Treats and Drinks

Early Medieval

Sugar was being processed in Persia as early as the sixth century. Despite no evidence of its existence in England during this time, there is an old adage that purports to the English monk the Venerable Bede bequeathing a morsel of sugar in his will of 735.[1] 'I take nothing for granted of this epoch, which widely enjoyed the spoils of trade including exotic spices, oils and wines, so why not sugar? Maybe.'

All evidence suggests that honey was the main source of sweetness in the early medieval era. There were also a variety of sweet herbs like marshmallow, galingale, anise, fennel and mint to name a few, which were worked into dishes as general sweeteners. Liquorice was probably one of the last naturally sweet plants to be introduced from the Mediterranean via China. There is certainly no known Old English word for it and its provenance is

Sugar cane.

Marshmallow plant.

debateable, ranging from the eleventh to the sixteenth centuries, found originally growing in the monasteries of the north of England.

It wasn't just the pleasing piquancy of this particular sense that made sweet things important to early medieval society when you consider that a mixture of sweet beets, mallow and cabbage boiled together in a pork broth was thought to sustain the function of the womb, and for kidney pains sweet wine combined with the herb betony and hot water was recommended as a medicinal drink.[2] There are many sweet-based remedies that appear in the leechdoms of the Anglo-Saxon age. Unbelievably, this totally unfounded belief that sugar, both natural and processed, was good for you and could alleviate a multitude of ailments lasted well into the nineteenth century.

Honey was also highly prized both as a culinary ingredient and as a substance used in rituals, for poultices and medicinal drinks.

Mead is the best known of all the ancient honey-based drinks, but Oxymel, originally drunk by the Greeks and Romans was also consumed during the early medieval period and is mentioned in *Bald's Leechbook,* which even provides us with a recipe:

> from vinegar and from honey; take the best honey, put it over the hearth, seethe away the wax and the scum, then add to the honey as much vinegar, so as that it may not be very austere nor very sweet; mingle together, and set by the fire in a crock, boil upon good gledes, clean and lively, till the mixture be mingled, so that it may be one, and have the thickness of honey, and on tasting it the austere sharpness of the vinegar may not be too evident.[3]

Aseneth offering bread, wine and honey to an angel, *c.* 1475. (Getty Museum)

A wassail represents a merging of both a customary drink and salutation to good health. One of its earliest written references appears in Geoffrey of Monmouth's twelfth century *Historia Regum Britanniae*, a documentation of Anglo-Saxon life, a translation of which reads: 'the daughter of Hengist, bearing a golden vessel full of wine ... bent on her knees.' The Saxon language says 'Washail, [vrr. Washeil, Weshail, Waesseil, wassheil], Lauert King.'[4]

Wassail was essentially born out of Norse pagan feasting and festivals, often associated with Christmas and New Year and frequently quoted as a derivative of the Old English *hǣl* or *hál* meaning safe and in good health. Wassail as a drink did not emerge until much later in the medieval period as a spiced, mulled customary and festive beverage, linked to sustaining the harvests and served up in a ceremonial cup.

In 2011 the remains of thousands of charred barley grains were excavated at a 2,000-year-old site in Eberdingen-Hochdorf, Germany. Archaeologists suspect this is evidence of high-quality barley malt production. The barley was soaked in ditches until it began to sprout, before being heated to add both a smoky aroma and rich hue. To increase fermentation, fruit or honey was possibly added together with herbs to increase flavour.

Eleventh to Thirteenth Centuries

Continuing with the theme of sugar as a restorative remedy, scribed by the Italian surgeon Lanfranc who practised medicine in France during the thirteenth century, the *Science of*

Wassail bowl. (© Emma Kay)

Ornate punch cup from the late 1700s. (© Emma Kay)

cirurgie was translated into Middle English and was widely disseminated across Europe at the time. It references both *Penidium* and *Diamoron*. Interestingly, the latter derives from the word *penide*, translating as barley sugar, formed into the shape of little pellets. The composition of barley water and sugar as a remedy for the lungs in this form predates a much later provenance for this mix, which is often attributed to France in the seventeenth century. It actually originated in the Middle East.[5]

Diamoron was a confection made of mulberries, recipes for which appear in multiple texts of the 1500s in England. According to the Oxford English Dictionary, the earliest recorded date for *Diamoron* is 1400.

The following recipe, which I have loosely translated, was published in William Bullein's *Defence Against All Sickness*.

> Take of the juice of mulberries and the juice of black berries and honey, sweet wine ... Take your juice, let it boil with your honey and sweet wine ... To know when it is well sodden you must take a drop of it and lay it upon a marble stone and it will abyde upon the stone and clear like thick honey ... Strain it and keep it in a vessel of tin. This is very good against sores in the throat and all kinds of strangling and pains in the mouth.[6]

Mulberries. (Courtesy of Karen Hine)

Having experimented with a few recipes for barley sugar both old and new, I reworked my own successful version:

Barley Sugar Twists
50 g pearl barley
1 litre of water
300 g of granulated sugar
The juice and rind of half a lemon

- Bring your barley, water and lemon rind to boiling point in a large, preferably non-stick pan. The size of the pan is important here as the boiling sugar mixture will rise considerably during cooking. Simmer on a very low heat for 45–60 minutes, then let it cool.
- Sieve the mix and discard the rind and barley. You should be left with about 400 ml of barley water.
- Clean out your pan and add the barley water and sugar. Simmer and stir gently until all the sugar has dissolved.
- Boil on a high heat until the temperature reaches 115°C on a sugar thermometer. This is a very important stage and you must remain patient until the mixture reaches the desired temperature. It's also important to keep stirring, so that the froth does not overflow. Take care with very hot sugar, which can burn.
- Once the sugar and water reach 115°C, carefully add the lemon juice. Continue to boil and stir until the temperature rises to 150°C.
- Remove the mixture from the heat and pour into a greased baking tray. Let it cool until it's safe to handle. This will only be a minute or two at the very most. It is important the mixture does not harden and remains pliable enough to be handled.
- Cut or just break off 5 cm odd short lengths of the confection and quickly twist each one into shape or any desired shape you want, but be quick as it will set very quickly indeed and you will be left with a big sheet of barley sugar.
- Place the finished barley twists onto baking paper and leave to cool completely.

Interestingly, most barley sugar recipes from the nineteenth century don't even include barley, a bit like the no-ginger gingerbread; they rely mostly on boiled sugar or boiled sugar and lemon, which is simply cut into strips and twisted before cooling. It would appear that by the end of the Georgian period the need to add the barley water itself had become redundant, perhaps because barley sugar became more associated with pleasure candy than medicinal confection.

A quick nod to blancmange is required in this section, which was a dish consisting of rice with shredded chicken or fish, almonds and sugar made popular in the fourteenth century – not the solid, milky, sweet jelly we typically associate with this pudding. However, its origins are much earlier, possibly deriving from the Danish *Hwit Moos* as recorded in the 1200s by Henrik Harpestaeng, which was a dish itself inspired by the ancient Arabic milk pudding *muhallabiyya* and undoubtedly consumed as some variation of the two during the earlier Anglo-Saxon era.

Basic barley sugar. (© Emma Kay)

White moos

Quomodo temperetur cibus qui uocatur hwit moos You must take sweet milk. and well writhet hwetebrøth. and scrambled eggs. and well written saffron. oc latæ dense wællæ to dense warthær thiuct. Sithen latæ tight up .a. disk. and throw .i. butter. oc strø .a. puluar of cinnamon. Dense heather white moos.

How to prepare something called white mash. You have to take whole milk, and well-crumbled wheat bread (crumbs), and beaten eggs, and well-grated saffron, and let it boil until it becomes thick. Then put it on a plate and add butter and sprinkle with cinnamon powder. It's called white moss.[7]

There remains a widespread belief that water wasn't drinkable during the medieval period. Research of the period to determine the amount of grain required to make ale, very clearly demonstrates that something in the region of over 80 per cent of the country's entire grain production during the medieval period would have had to be used to make enough ale to serve the whole population. Clearly, this was an impossibility, as grain was largely

Recreation of white moos. (© Emma Kay)

required for food. The germ theory wasn't discovered until the nineteenth century, which also begs the question why anyone living in the medieval age would even consider water to be polluted. Rural populations had abundant access to fresh water supplies in streams and wells and its likely they drank it in large quantities, along with some weak ales.

Wine was both imported from countries including Spain, France and Greece and produced in local vineyards, of which England had many, established by the Romans and sustained by the Anglo-Saxons.

The *c.* 1370 text of Piers Ploughman refers to a drink from apples, possibly a type of cider: 'May no pyement ne pomade ne presiouse drynkes Moyste me to the fulle ne my thurst slake.'[8] While the Old English word *æppelwin* of the Anglo-Saxon era also translates as apple cider.[9]

Pressing wine after the harvest. (From *Tacuinum Sanitatis*, fourteenth century)

Bragot, braggot, bragett, braget or bracket was a sort of ale and honey brew, the origins of which have been distorted over the centuries. Bragot is often associated with the ancient words *bracata* and *bracis*, but these are not Old English words. They have been linked to the Celtic language and appear to be more Latin based to me. The combination of grains and honey in brewing is certainly an ancient process, but one of the earliest references I can find for bragot is as late as the mid-1300s in the historical and theological chronicle *Polychronicon* written by the Benedictine monk Ranulf Higden, where he remarks: 'Of braget [bragotte], meth, and ale Is grete plente in þat vale.'[10]

Bragot is also mentioned in Chaucer's *Miller's Tale* of 1390: 'Hir mouth was swete as bragot or the meeth.'[11]

The additional references to both meth and meeth may relate to *Metheglin*, a type of flavoured mead also attributed to the Welsh as a term for 'healing liquor'.

Ginger offered an alternative in its sweet, preserved form. The following recipe is one that was discovered amongst the '*salsamenta*' of the eleventh-century Durham Cathedral manuscripts:

Preserved Ginger

Preserved ginger is made in order to stimulate the urge for sexual intercourse, and to strengthen digestion. Take the roots and cook them well, and chop up the cooked roots very finely and squeeze out the water. Form into small balls, add skimmed honey and cook until the honey is reduced, and stir continuously so that it does not stick to the pot. Midway through the cooking, add almonds (if you have them) and at the end, hulled pine-nuts, and afterwards aromatic spices: ginger, galingale, pepper, nutmeg and other aromatic spices.[12]

This type of candied preserve was undoubtedly the inspiration for Suckets or from the French *succades* or fruits preserved in sugar. There were wet syrup stored and dried candied suckets, many of which were often imported from countries like Spain and Portugal.

There were even sucket forks manufactured around the seventeenth century with prongs to spear your sucket and a spoon the other end to eat it with, like a contemporary spork.

The addition of sugar in wealthier households made for other luxuries like quince marmalade and fruit pastes, all alternative forms of conserving fresh fruit as a sweet year-round treat, treats that would undoubtedly have been served at grand estates.

Sweetmeats form a very wide category of medieval candied/crystallised fruits or other confections/comfits, like sugar plums, dragees (sugared almonds), sucades, pionads (containing peony seeds), pynenade/pynyonades (sweetmeats with pinenuts) and so on. Sugar was boiled to reach a high concentration syrup – what some confectioners call the soft ball stage – before either being rolled or mixed with an assortment of seeds, fruits, nuts and spices. Originating in the Middle East, these confections served as both medicinal remedies and as victuals to be enjoyed after a meal, just as they would over time across Europe. The following recipe dates to around the twelfth century.

Crystallised ginger. (© Emma Kay)

Caramelised and plain almonds. (© Emma Kay)

Khabîs al-lauz.

Take one ratl [about 450 g] of peeled, ground sweet almonds and three ratls (just over 1 kg) of sugar. Put the sugar in a dish and dissolve, with two uqiya [about 50 ml] of rose-water. When the sugar is dissolved and has begun to set, add the ground almonds, and stir until done. Serve out, coating under and over with fine-ground sugar. This may also be made with flour: put with the ratl of sugar two uqiya of flour, then proceed as above. *A Baghdad Cookery Book* (Kitāb al-Ṭabīkh).[13]

The history of gingerbread is complex, but the earliest reference I can find appears in the calendar rolls of Henry III in 1228, which simply mentions 'gingebrad'.[14]

Initial recipes for gingerbread consisted of marzipan heavily spiced with ginger, while 'red gingerbread', first attributed to York, could have been made using red wine or a food colouring like sandalwood. It certainly would not have resembled the cakey gingerbread we are familiar with today.

As the period progressed there was a shift from gingered marzipan to a breadcrumb and honey paste of spices and, quite often, no actual ginger. Medieval gingerbread, like many victuals prepared by the wealthy, was lavish, showy and medicinal. In their medieval compilation *Curye on Inglysch*, Constance Hieatt and Sharon Butler draw a persuasive and definitive line between gingerbread confection and gingerbread as a cake, with the inclusion of this gingerbread confection recipe I have translated from the turn of the 1300s, found in the British Library manuscript Add.46919 *Diuersa Cibaria* (Diverse Foodstuffs):

Gingerbread cake. (© Emma Kay)

By way of Cyprus

Of almond milk, rice flour, powdered ginger, so that it tastes a lot of ginger and that it be sprinkled with pistachios.[15]

Late Medieval

Wafers were first mentioned in relation to religious ceremonies and even earlier as pagan rituals, like this one to rid a person of warts translated from the tenth-century medical texts collectively known as *Lacnunga* (Remedies):

> Against a warty eruption, one must take seven little wafers, such as a man offereth with, and write these names on each wafer, Maximianus, Malchus, Iohannes, Martinianus, Dionysius, Constantinus, Sera-fion; then again one must sing the charm which is hereinafter mentioned, first into the left ear, then into the right ear, then above the mans poll, then let one who is a maiden go to him and hang it upon his neck, do so for three days, it will soon be well with him.[16]

Communion wafers or oublies/obleys eventually evolved into the waffle a light-batter-type cake popular throughout the later medieval period in France, Belgium, Holland and Germany. They became a luxury dessert item with the rise in the production of sugar.

Wafers became more diverse as time went on, with those containing cheese restyling themselves as popular street food by the sixteenth century.

Communion wafers.

Although obleys appear in earlier medieval recipes, including the fourteenth-century *Forme of Cury*, it's generally considered that the word 'waffle' didn't appear in print in England until 1725 with the publication of Robert Smith's *Court Cookery*.

Waffles and wafers exist all over the world in a variety of forms, and there are too many to mention here. The Belgian waffle (actually an American term, based on the Brussels waffle) has become one of the most popular, with its large, deep honeycomb squares often accompanied by fruit and cream. The legacy of the oublie lives on as the *oblea* variation, a sweet wafer dessert to be found in Spain and Latin American countries today, commonly filled with *delce de leche*.

The traditional sponge cake mix of flour, fat, eggs and sugar didn't materialise until the very end of the medieval period in England, on the cusp of the 1600s, with one of the very first recipes of this type published in Thomas Dawson's *The Good Huswifes Jewell*.

Medieval 'cakes' consisted of anything formed into a cake shape. One of the earliest recorded, in John Gower's *Confessio Amantis* of the mid-1300s, is the simple barley cake.[17]

From flour and seeds to cheese and almonds, which might be baked, boiled or fried, cakes certainly didn't have to be sweet. One such savoury cake was the hugely popular tansy cake, mostly eaten for their medicinal properties and the herb's alleged ability to kill intestinal worms. As such, they were frequently enjoyed at Easter following the period of Lent when the amount of fish consumed as an alternative to meat could generate outbreaks of worms.[18]

The serving of the void in which wine, wafers and spices were consumed during important ceremonies to aid digestion evolved within the context of the elaborate banquets of the Elizabethan age.

The foundations of dessert as we know it began with this medieval 'void', when fruit, jellies and other sweetmeats were eaten standing up and away from the dining hall, which

Rolled wafers. (© Emma Kay)

Tansy herb.

allowed the room to be cleared for any after-dinner activities. This ritual granted dessert a detached quality, giving way to creativity and flamboyance and the emergence of elaborate sugar works, or 'subtleties' as they were called, which could also be sculptured in pastry. The bigger the artwork, the larger your demonstration of wealth.

In 1526 Henry VIII allegedly hired seven cooks at Greenwich to create a sugar banquet, including a dungeon and a manor house with swans as well as a tower and chessboard, all covered in gold.

Marzipan, or marchpane, a combination of ground almonds and sugar beaten into a paste, was ideal for crafting subtleties as it was firm, pliable and smooth all at the same time, so it could also be gilded with gold leaf for extra decadence. Confections like marzipan, which either originated in the Mediterranean or Asia, were favoured in the Tudor court. Despite this confection having a much earlier provenance, it isn't mentioned much before the 1500s in England.

Then there were endless varieties of spiced, sweetened and fruited cakes and breads to add depth and flavour. One was wigs/whigs (meaning 'wedge-shaped'), which may have been a Dutch influence of the 1300s, while sugar, the new medieval drug of the wealthy, was added to meat and egg dishes too. Florentines are an excellent example of a recipe that has altered dramatically over the last 500 years. Similar to the mince pie, which slowly discarded the meat element over time, those loveable chocolate-coated fruit and nut slightly caramelly discs, Florentines were once put together with minced bits of offal, various meats, suet, eggs, dates and spices, like this recipe from the 1500s:

To make Florentines

Take Vele and some of the Kidney of the Loyne, or colde Veale roasted, colde capon or Phesant, which of them you wil, and mince it very small with sweet suet, put unto

Making marchpane during a demonstration. (© Emma Kay)

Florentines. (© Emma Kay)

it two or three yolks of Egs, being hard sod, Corance and dates small shred, season it with a little sinamon and ginger, a very little cloves and mace, with a little Salte and sugar, a little Time being finely shred. Make your paste fine with butter & yolkes of Egs and Sugar, role it very thin and so lay it in a platter with butter underneath: and so cut your cover and lay it upon it.[19]

Another likely candidate for the Tudor banqueting table was the daryol, or custard tart. A recipe appears in *The Forme of Cury* (1390):

Daryols/dariol
Take Creme of Cowe mylke. oþer of Almandes. do þerto ayren with sugur, safroun, and salt, medle it yfere. do it in a coffyn. of II. ynche depe. bake it wel and serue it forth.[20]

Custard Tarts (my translation)
Take cream of cow milk, other of almonds, add that to egg with sugar, saffron and salt, mix it together and add it to a coffin (pastry case) two inches deep and serve it forth.

A medieval crab apple paste called chardecrab was also made with quinces. Chardequince involved boiling, straining and heating chopped quince with honey and spices before being boxed and stored for a couple of months in a cool place. It is often defined as a precursor to marmalade, as quince pastes and jellies are historically intrinsic to the evolution of this modern conserve.

Chardequince
Take quinces and divide in four pieces with a knife, and take the flesh separated from the pips and boil it in a pan with clear water until it is very soft, then remove from the fire and strain through the middle of a strainer or sieve; and if there are 8 pounds of flesh, add 6 pounds of clarified honey, and put it over the fire and let it boil stirring continuously until it is completely cooked, and test it in this way: take a knife, and take some of the mixture on the point of the knife and let it cool, if it is stiff, then it is cooked enough. Then remove from the fire and stir well until it begins to turn white; then add two pounds of eringo powder, 3 ounces of ginger, very finely chopped, and 6 ounces of ground ginger, and put all this combined into boxes and keep until needed.[21]

Furmenty/Frumenty/furmity/firmenty
This was a thick medieval porridge that was often made of cracked wheat. Its name derives from the Latin *frumentum*, meaning grain.

It was traditionally eaten during Lent as it contained no meat, but it was sometimes served alongside meat or meat stews. *The Forme of Cury* dictates that furmenty was most popular served alongside venison in the 1300s.

It became a dish that straddled all classes, and as the medieval period progressed it became synonymous with celebrations and family get togethers. Furmenty was often something to be enjoyed at parish gatherings, feasts and festivals. It was, in my opinion,

Quinces.

Quince jelly. (© Emma Kay)

the forerunner to the Christmas plum porridge and eventually the plum pudding, as dried fruit and alcohol became additional staple ingredients over the following centuries.

A recipe for furmenty appears in the English manuscript Douce 257 compiled around 1381, but many other variations can be found in other medieval culinary manuscripts, including those from France and Italy:

> **Furmenty**
> Nym clene wete & bray it in a morter wel, þat þe holys gon al of, & seyt yt til yt breste; & nym yt vp & lat it kele. And nym fayre fresch broþ & swete mylk of almandys or swete mylk of kyne and temper yt al. & nym þe olkys of eyryn & saffron & do þerto. Boyle it a lityl & set yt adoun, & messe yt forþe wyþ fat venysoun & fresch motoun.[22]
>
> My own translation:
> Take clean, soaked wheat which has been ground in a mortar, crack and pierce it [the grains] until they burst and take it, turn it upright and let it cool. And take good, clean fresh broth and sweet milk of almonds or sweet milk of cows and mix it all and take the yolks of eggs & saffron and add it all together. Boil it a little & set it down and serve it forthwith with venison and fresh mutton.

By the 1700s it became commonplace to add sugar, currants and/or raisins to frumenty if you were lucky enough to afford them. One such recipe cane be found in Hannah Glasse's famed cookery book *The Art of Cookery Made Plain and Easy*:

> Take two quarts of hull'd, boiled wheat, a gallon of milk, two quarts of cream, and boil them till they are pretty thick, then put in sugar, the yolks of eight or ten eggs well beaten, three pounds of currants, plump'd by being gently boil'd in water: Put these into the furmity, give them a few Warms, and it will be done.[23]

Mulled wines, ciders and fruit juices were incredibly popular throughout the Middle Ages at a time when coffee, tea and chocolate drinks were still at least a century away. Caudles were thick, warm and soothing drinks prepared for the sick. They have a legacy that extends to at least the thirteenth century and continued well into the Victorian age when it had evolved into a specific custom for new mothers. Caudle cups designed for these drinks remained popular from the 1600s onwards. The following recipe is from *The Good Huswifes Jewell* of 1596.

> To make a Caudle to comfort the stomacke, good for an old man.
> Take a pinte of good Muscadine, and as much of good stale ale, mingle them together, then take the yolkes of twelue or thirteene Egges newe laide, beat well the Egges firste by themselues, with the wine and ale, and so boyle it together, and

Furmenty with dried fruit and spices. (© Emma Kay)

> put thereto a quarterne of Suger, and a fewe whole Mace, and so stirre it well, til it seeth a good while, and when it is well sod, put therin a few slices of bread if you will, and so let it soke a while, and it will be right good and wholesome.[24]

One of the most popular drinks of the fifteenth century was the posset, made with curdled milk and either wine or ale mixed with sugar and spices. The dish was reinvented as a sweet pudding in the nineteenth century and is better known as a cold set dessert today, a little like a syllabub. The diarist Samuel Pepys mentions posset with some frequency in his famous memoirs, but is more often referring to sack-posset, the fortified sherry wine of Spain.

This is my own posset recipe, inspired by both the medieval and more familiar modern-day versions.

Lemon and Ginger Posset
(Serves 3)
270 ml double cream
120 g caster sugar
30 ml limoncello
½ teaspoon powdered ginger
Candied ginger to decorate

- Put the cream and sugar in a saucepan, heat gently and stir to dissolve the sugar. Simmer gently for a minute or two. Take the cream and sugar mix off the heat. Stir in the limoncello and the powdered ginger. You may find that the ginger clumps together and is hard to combine. Just persevere with vigorous stirring and it will eventually mix in.

- Pour the mixture into small glasses or pots, leave to cool before chilling overnight (or at least 4 hours) in the refrigerator.
- Once set, decorate each posset with a little candied ginger.

Mead is Scandinavian in origin and while it has almost become a culinary cliché of the medieval age, I felt compelled to include a short recipe here from the 1600s Danish *Kogebog* (cookbook) which is based on another publication, *Oeconomia oder Hausbuch* (Economies of the House) by Johann Coler, compiled around 1593.

> **White mead to make, that will be used soon**
> Take one measure white honey and eight measures fresh spring water. Let this seethe [boil] together 4 hours and scum it well. [remove the scum] You must not make it too thick. Let it then stand to cool. Thereafter sieve it through a Lutendrancks bag [straining bag] with herbs, cinnamon, cardamom, cubeb [a little like allspice] galingale, grains of paradise, [related to cardamon] ginger, long pepper and cloves.[25]

The drinking of mead in the mead hall was a highly ceremonial process in the Anglo-Saxon era and similar etiquette continued to dominate the tables of the wealthy during the later medieval period. Even today, customs like the top table at a wedding or sitting the most prominent or senior guest at the head of the table and requesting they carve the roast meat during mealtimes prevails. Along with many of the familiar dishes included in this book – from blancmange and barley sugar to rissoles and quiche – it's an indicator that history is never as far removed as we often think.

Lemon and ginger posset. (© Emma Kay)

Home-brewed mead. (© Emma Kay)

John, Duke of Berry enjoys a grand meal, sitting at the high table in front of the fireplace, served by a carver and other servants. On the table to the duke's left is a golden salt cellar, or nef, in the shape of a ship. (*Tres Riches Heures du Duc de Berry*, c. 1410)

Notes

Chapter 1: Soups, Stews, Breads and Dough

1. Vehling, J., *De Re Coquinaria, or Apicius* (Walter Hill: 1936).
2. St Hildegard, *Hildegard Von Bingen's Physica: The Complete English Translation of Her Classic Work on Health and Healing* (Healing Arts Press: Canada, 1998), p.194.
3. al-Muẓaffar ibn Naṣr Ibn Sayyār al-Warrāq, Saḥbān Murūwah, *Annals of the Caliphs' Kitch ens, Ibn Sayyār Al-Warrāq's Tenth-century Baghdadi Cookbook* (Brill: The Netherlands, 2007).
4. Hieatt, C. B., *The Culinary Recipes of Medieval England* (Prospect Books: Devon, 2013), p.33.
5. Chaucer, G., Morris, R. (ed.), *The Prologue, the Knightes Tale, the Nonne Preestes Tale, from the Canterbury Tales* (Clarendon Press: Oxford, 1889), p.154.
6. Morris, Richard, *Liber Cure Cocorum* (A. Asher & Co.: Berlin, 1862).
7. Furnivall, F. J. (ed.), *The babees book, Aristotle's A B C, Urbanitatis, Stans puer ad mensam, The lvtille childrenes lvtil boke, The bokes of nurture of Hugh Rhodes and John Russell, Wynkyn de Worde's Boke of keruynge, The booke of demeanor, The boke of curtasye, Seager's Schoole of vertue, &c. &c. with some French and latin poems on like subjects, and some forewords on education in early England* (Early English Text Society: London, 1868).
8. Parker, Eleanor, *Winters in the World. A Journey through the Anglo-Saxon year* (Reaktion Books Ltd: London, 2022).
9. Cummins, P. W., *A Critical Edition of Le Regime Tresutile et Tresproufitable pour Conserver et Garder la Santé du Corps Humain* (North Carolina Studies in the Romance Languages and Literatures: Chapel Hill, 1976).
10. Hammond, P., *Food & Feast in Medieval England* (The History Press: Stroud, 2017).
11. Hanawait, B., *Crime in East Anglia in the Fourteenth Century* (Norfolk Record Society: 1976), p.14.
12. Burton, H., *Cannibalism in High Medieval English Literature* (Palgrave Macmillan: New York, 2016).
13. British Library, Harley MS 2378, bl.uk, accessed 4 December 2022.

14. British Newspaper Library, *North Bucks Times and County Observer* (Saturday 4 November 1893).
15. Simpson, J., Roud, S., *A Dictionary of English Folklore* (OUP: Oxford, 2003).
16. Russell, John, Furnivall, Frederick, J. (ed.), *Boke of Nurture in Early English Meals and Manners* (OUP: London, 1868).
17. Toussaint-Samat,M., *A History of Food* (Wiley-Blackwell: Sussex, France, 2009).
18. Rabisher, W., *The Whole Body of Cookery* (London, 1675).
19. Austin, T., *Two Fifteenth-Century Cookery-Books* (OUP: London, New York, Toronto, 1888), p.46.
20. Pegge, S. (ed.), *The Forme of Cury* (J. Nichols: 1780).
21. Kay, E., *A History of British Baking* (Pen & Sword Books Ltd: 2020), p.83.
22. Bickley, F. R. (ed.), *The little red book of Bristol,* Vols 1 and 2 (Hemmons: Bristol, 1900), p.33.
23. Myers, D. (ed.), *Recipes from John Crophill's Commonplace Book* (Daniel Myers: 2016), p.13.
24. Morris, Richard, *Liber Cure Cocorum* (A. Asher & Co.: Berlin, 1862).

Chapter 2: Meat, Fish and Sauces

1. Cockayne, Oswald, *Leechdoms, wortcunning, and starcraft of early England. Being a collection of documents, for the most part never before printed, illustrating the history of science in this country before the Norman* Conquest, Volume 2 (Longman Green: London, 1864).
2. Kay, E., *Fodder and Drincan: Anglo-Saxon Culinary History* (Prospect Books: London, 2022), p.56.
3. Ensminger, Eugene, *Beef Cattle Science* (Interstate Printers and Publishers: USA, 1987), p.72.
4. Cockayne, Oswald, *Leechdoms, wortcunning, and starcraft of early England. Being a collection of documents, for the most part never before printed, illustrating the history of science in this country before the Norman* Conquest, Volume 2 (Longman Green: London, 1864).
5. Holmes, M., 'Southern England: A Review of Animal Remains from Saxon, Medieval and Post-Medieval Archaeological Sites', *Historic England Research Report Series,* No. 8, (2017).
6. Kay, E., *Fodder and Drincan: Anglo-Saxon Culinary History* (Prospect Books: London, 2022), p.49.
7. *Ibid,* p.80.
8. Martinelli, C. (ed.), *The Anonymous Andalusian Cookbook* (CreateSpace Independent Publishing Platform: 2012), p.83.
9. *Ibid,* p.64.
10. Taylor, J. (ed.), *The Didascalicon of Hugh of St. Victor: A Medieval Guide to the Arts* (New York and London: Columbia University Press, 1961), p.78.
11. Fowler, J. T., *Extracts from the account rolls of the Abbey of Durham,* Vol. 1 Durham Cathedral (1833–1924).

12. Austin, T., *Two Fifteenth-Century Cookery-Books* (OUP: London, New York, Toronto, 1888), p.75.
13. Warner, R. Rev., *Antiquitates Culinarie or Curious Tracts relating to the culinary affairs of the Old English* (London: 1791), p.70.
14. An Anglo-Saxon Dictionary Online, bosworthtoller.com, accessed 2 October 2021.
15. al-Muẓaffar ibn Naṣr Ibn Sayyār al-Warrāq, bān Murūwah, *Annals of the Caliphs' Kitch ens, Ibn Sayyār Al-Warrāq's Tenth-century Baghdadi Cookbook* (Brill: The Netherlands, 2007), p.196.
16. Hill, W., *De Re Coquinaria, or Apicius* (1936).
17. Giles, G., Wallis, F., 'Salsamenta pictavensium: Gastronomy and Medicine in Twelfth-Century England', *English Historical Review*, Volume 131 (2017), pp.1,353–85.
18. Power, E. (trans.), *The Goodman of Paris* (The Boydell Press: Woodbridge, 2006), p.188.
19. Chevallier, J., *How to Cook a Golden Peacock* (Chez Jim Books: North Hollywood, 2012).
20. Libellus De Arte Coquinaria, Wikipedia, accessed 16 January 2023.
21. Dawson, T., Myers, D. (trans.), *The Good Huswifes Jewell* (2008), medieval.com.
22. Austin, T., *Two Fifteenth-Century Cookery-Books* (OUP: London, New York, Toronto, 1888).
23. Morris, Richard, *Liber Cure Cocorum* (A. Asher & Co.: Berlin, 1862).

Chapter 3: Dairy, Eggs, Fruit and Veg

1. Chevallier, J., *How to Cook an Early French Peacock* (Chez Jim Books: 2021).
2. Anderson, R. (ed.), *The Elder Edda of Saemund Sigfusson and the Younger Edda of Snorre Sturleson* (Norroena Society: London, 1906).
3. Neckam, A., *De naturis rerum,* edited by Thomas Wright (Cambridge University Press, 1883).
4. Salvago, L., Umberto, A., *Was the English medieval goat genuinely rare? A new morphometric approach provides the answer* (Archaeological and Anthropological Sciences: 2019).
5. Vehling, J., *De Re Coquinaria, or Apicius* (Walter Hill: 1936).
6. Cummins, P. W., *A Critical Edition of Le Regime Tresutile et Tresproufitable pour Conserver et Garder la Santé du Corps Humain* (North Carolina Studies in the Romance Languages and Literatures: Chapel Hill, 1976).
7. Hieatt, C. B., Grewe, R. (ed.), *Libellus de arte coquinaria: An Early Northern Cookery Book* (Arizona Centre for Medieval and Renaissance Studies: 2009).
8. Libellus De Arte Coquinaria, Wikipedia, accessed 16 January 2023.
9. Giles, G., Wallis, F., 'Salsamenta pictavensium: Gastronomy and Medicine in Twelfth-Century England', *English Historical Review*, Volume 131 (2017), p.40.
10. Greco, G., Rose, C., *The Good Wife's Guide. Le Menagier de Paris* (Cornell University: 2009), p.320.
11. al-Muẓaffar ibn Naṣr Ibn Sayyār al-Warrāq, Saḥbān Murūwah, *Annals of the Caliphs' Kitch ens, Ibn Sayyār Al-Warrāq's Tenth-century Baghdadi Cookbook* (Brill: The Netherlands, 2007), p.110.
12. Hieatt, C., Butler, S., *Curye on Inglysch* (Oxford University Press: London, New York, Toronto, 1985).

13. A. W., *A Book of Cookrye* (Edward Allde: London, 1591).
14. Young, A., *Annals of Agriculture, Vol. 32* (J. Rackham: Bury St Edmunds, 1799).
15. Pringle, D., *Churches of the Crusader Kingdom* (Cambridge University Press: Cambridge, 1998).
16. Austin, T., *Two Fifteenth-Century Cookery-Books* (OUP: London, New York, Toronto, 1888).
17. Kay, E., *Fodder and Drincan: Anglo-Saxon Culinary History* (Prospect Books: London, 2022).
18. Cockayne, Oswald, *Leechdoms, wortcunning, and starcraft of early England. Being a collection of documents, for the most part never before printed, illustrating the history of science in this country before the Norman* Conquest, Volumes 1–3 (Longman Green, London, 1864).
19. Neckam, A., *De naturis rerum,* edited by Thomas Wright (Cambridge University Press, 1883).
20. Martinelli, C., (ed.), *The Anonymous Andalusian Cookbook* (CreateSpace Independent Publishing Platform: 2012), p.55.
21. Murrell, J., *A New Booke of Cookerie; London Cookerie* (London, 1615).
22. Pegge, S. (ed.), *The Forme of Cury* (J. Nichols, 1780).
23. Crieghton, C., *A History of Epidemics in Britain* (e-artnow: 2020).

Chapter 4: Sweet Treats and Drinks

1. Mintz, S., *Sweetness and Power: The Place of Sugar in Modern History* (Penguin Books: London, 1986), p.74.
2. Cockayne, Oswald, *Leechdoms, wortcunning, and starcraft of early England. Being a collection of documents, for the most part never before printed, illustrating the history of science in this country before the Norman* conquest, Volume 2 (Longman Green: London, 1864).
3. *Ibid.*
4. Hammer, J. (ed.), *Geoffrey of Monmouth, Historia Regum Britanniae* (1951).
5. Fleischhacker, R. V., *Lanfrank's 'Science of cirurgie'*, edited from the Bodleian Ashmole ms. 1396 (ab. 1380 A.D.) and the British Museum additional ms. 12,056 (ab. 1420 A.D.).
6. Bullein, W., *Bulleins Bulwarke of Defence Against All Sicknesse, Soarenesse, and Woundes that Doe Dayly Assaulte Mankinde* (Thomas Marsh: London, 1579).
7. Libellus De Arte Coquinaria, Wikipedia, accessed 16 January 2023.
8. Skeat, W. W. (ed.), *The Vision of William Concerning Piers the Plowman, part 3* (Early English Text Society, Original Series 54, 1873).
9. Old English to Modern English Translator, oldenglishtranslator.co.uk, accessed 05 December 2022.
10. Babington, C., Lumby, J. R. (eds), *Polychronicon Ranulphi Higden,* 8 Vols, Rolls Series (Rerum Britannicarum Medii Aevi Scriptores) (1865–86), p.41.
11. Manly, J. M., Rickert, E., *The Text of the Canterbury Tales* (Chicago, 1940).
12. Giles, G., Wallis, F., 'Salsamenta pictavensium: Gastronomy and Medicine' in 'Twelfth-Century England', *English Historical Review,* Volume 131 (2017), p.44.

13. Perry, C. (trans.) *A Baghdad Cookery Book (Kitāb al-Ṭabīkh)* (Prospect Books: 2005).
14. Calendar of the Liberate Rolls Preserved in the Public Record Office, Henry III, AD 1226–1240, Vol. 1 (1916).
15. Hieatt, C., Butler, S., *Curye on Inglysch* (Oxford University Press: London, New York, Toronto, 1985).
16. Cockayne, Oswald, *Leechdoms, wortcunning, and starcraft of early England. Being a collection of documents, for the most part never before printed, illustrating the history of science in this country before the Norman* Conquest, Volume 3 (Longman Green: London, 1864).
17. Gower, J., *Confessio amantis* (Clarendon Press: Oxford, 1899–1902).
18. Kay, E., *A History of British Baking* (Pen & Sword Books Ltd: 2020), p.30.
19. A. W., *A Book of Cookrye* (Edward Allde: London, 1591).
20. Pegge, S. (ed.) *The Forme of Cury* (J. Nichols: 1780).
21. Banham, D., Mason, L., *Confectionery Recipes from a Fifteenth-century Manuscript* (Petits Propos Culinaires: 2002).
22. Hieatt, C., Butler, S., *Curye on Inglysch* (Oxford University Press: London, New York, Toronto, 1985).
23. Glasse, H., *The New Art of Cookery, Made Plain and Easy, Etc* (John Exshaw: Dublin, 1762), p.135.
24. Dawson, T., Myers, D. (trans.), *The Good Huswifes Jewell* (2008), medieval.com.
25. *Koge Bog*, online translation by Martin Forest, forest.gen.nz/Medieval/articles/cooking/1616.html, accessed 5 January 2023.

Bibliography

A. W., *A Book of Cookrye* (Edward Allde: London, 1591).

al-Muẓaffar ibn Naṣr Ibn Sayyār al-Warrāq, Saḥbān Murūwah, *Annals of the Caliphs' Kitchens: Ibn Sayyār Al-Warrāq's Tenth-century Baghdadi Cookbook* (Brill: The Netherlands, 2007).

Anderson, R. (ed.), *The Elder Edda of Saemund Sigfusson and the Younger Edda of Snorre Sturleson* (London: Norroena Society, 1906).

Austin, T., *Two Fifteenth-Century Cookery-Books* (OUP: London, New York, Toronto, 1888).

Babington, C., Lumby, J. R. (eds), *Polychronicon Ranulphi Higden*, Vol. 8, Rolls Series (Rerum Britannicarum Medii Aevi Scriptores, 1865–86), p.41.

Banham, D., Mason, L., *Confectionery Recipes from a Fifteenth-century Manuscript* (Petits Propos Culinaires, p.69 (2002).

Bickley, F. R. (ed.), *The Little Red Book of Bristol*, Vols 1 and 2 (Hemmons: Bristol, 1900).

Bullein, W., *Bulleins Bulwarke of Defence Against All Sicknesse, Soarenesse, and Woundes that Doe Dayly Assaulte Mankinde* (Thomas Marsh: London, 1579).

Burton, H., *Cannibalism in High Medieval English Literature* (Palgrave Macmillan: New York, 2016).

Calendar of the Liberate Rolls Preserved in the Public Record Office, Henry III, AD 1226–1240, Vol. 1 (1916).

Chaucer, G., Morris, R. (ed), *The Prologue, the Knightes Tale, the Nonne Preestes Tale, from the Canterbury Tales* (Clarendon Press: Oxford, 1889).

Chevallier, J., *How to Cook a Golden Peacock* (Chez Jim Books: North Hollywood, 2012).

Chevallier, J, *How to Cook an Early French Peacock* (Chez Jim Books: 2021).

Cockayne, Oswald, *Leechdoms, wortcunning, and starcraft of early England. Being a collection of documents, for the most part never before printed, illustrating the history of science in this country before the Norman* conquest, Vols 1–3 (Longman Green: London, 1864).

Crieghton, C., *A History of Epidemics in Britain* (e-artnow: 2020).

Cummins, P. W., *A Critical Edition of Le Regime Tresutile et Tresproufitable pour Conserver et Garder la Santé du Corps Humain* (North Carolina Studies in the Romance Languages and Literatures: Chapel Hill, 1976).

Dawson, T., Myers, D. (trans.), *The Good Huswifes Jewell* (2008), medieval.com.

Ensminger, Eugene, *Beef Cattle Science* (Interstate Printers and Publishers, USA, 1987).

Fleischhacker, R.V., Lanfrank's "Science of cirurgie". Edited from the Bodleian Ashmole ms. 1396 (ab. 1380 A.D.) and the British museum Additional ms. 12,056 (ab. 1420 A.D.)

Fowler, J. T., *Extracts From the Account Rolls of the Abbey of Durham,* Vol. 1 Durham Cathedral (1833–1924).

Furnivall, F. J. (ed.), *The babees book, Aristotle's A B C, Urbanitatis, Stans puer ad mensam, The lvtille childrenes lvtil boke, The bokes of nurture of Hugh Rhodes and John Russell, Wynkyn de Worde's Boke of keruynge, The booke of demeanor, The boke of curtasye, Seager's Schoole of vertue, &c. &c. with some French and latin poems on like subjects, and some forewords on education in early England* (Early English Text Society: London, 1868).

Giles, G., Wallis, F., 'Salsamenta pictavensium: Gastronomy and Medicine in Twelfth-Century England', *English Historical Review,* Volume 131 (2017).

Glasse, H., *The New Art of Cookery, Made Plain and Easy, Etc* (John Exshaw: Dublin, 1762).

Gower, J., *Confessio amantis* (Oxford: Clarendon Press, 1899–1902).

Greco, G., Rose, C., *The Good Wife's Guide. Le Menagier de Paris* (Cornell University: 2009).

Halliwell-Phillips, J. O., *A Dictionary of Archaic and Provincial Words, Obsolete Phrases, Proverbs, and Ancient Customs, from the Fourteenth Century,* Volume 1 (John Russell Smith: London, 1878).

Hammer, J. (ed.), *Geoffrey of Monmouth, Historia Regum Britanniae* (1951).

Hammond, P., *Food & Feast in Medieval England* (The History Press: Stroud, 2017).

Hanawait, B., *Crime in East Anglia in the Fourteenth Century* (Norfolk Record Society: 1976).

Hieatt, C. B., *The Culinary Recipes of Medieval England* (Prospect Books: Devon, 2013).

Hieatt, C., Butler, S., *Curye on Inglysch* (Oxford University Press: London, New York, Toronto, 1985).

Hieatt, C. B., Grewe, R. (ed.), *Libellus de arte coquinaria: An Early Northern Cookery Book* (Arizona Centre for Medieval and Renaissance Studies: 2009).

Hill, W., *De Re Coquinaria, or Apicius* (1936).

Holmes, M., 'Southern England: A Review of Animal Remains from Saxon, Medieval and Post-Medieval Archaeological Sites', *Historic England Research Report Series,* No. 8, (2017).

Kay, E., *A History of British Baking* (Pen & Sword Books Ltd: 2020).

Kay, E., *Fodder and Drincan: Anglo-Saxon Culinary History* (Prospect Books: London, 2022).

Manly, J. M., Rickert, E., *The Text of the Canterbury Tales* (Chicago, 1940).

Martinelli, C. (ed.), *The Anonymous Andalusian Cookbook* (CreateSpace Independent Publishing Platform: 2012).

Martirosyan, H., *The Mysterious Armenian Gata and its Ancient Origins* (Yerevan Physics Institute, 2021).

McIntosh Marjorie Keniston, *Poor Relief in England, 1350–1600* (Cambridge University Press: 2011).

Mintz, S., *Sweetness and Power: The Place of Sugar in Modern History* (London: Penguin Books, 1986).

Morris, Richard, *Liber Cure Cocorum* (A. Asher & Co.: Berlin, 1862).

Murrell, J., *A New Booke of Cookerie; London Cookerie* (London, 1615).

Myers, D., (ed) *Recipes from John Crophill's Commonplace Book* (Daniel Myers, 2016).

Neckam, A., *De naturis rerum,* edited by Thomas Wright (Cambridge University Press: 1883).

Parker, Eleanor, *Winters in the World: A Journey Through the Anglo-Saxon Year* (Reaktion Books Ltd: London, 2022).

Pegge, S. (ed.), *The Forme of Cury,* (J. Nichols: 1780).

Perry, C. (trans.), *A Baghdad Cookery Book (Kitāb al-Ṭabīkh)* (Prospect Books: 2005).

Pringle, D., *Churches of the Crusader Kingdom* (Cambridge University Press: Cambridge, 1998).

Power, E. (trans.), *The Goodman of Paris* (The Boydell Press: Woodbridge, 2006).

Rabisher, W., *The Whole Body of Cookery* (London, 1675).

Russell, John, Furnivall, Frederick, J. (ed.), *Boke of Nurture in Early English Meals and Manners* (OUP: London, 1868).

St Hildegard, *Hildegard Von Bingen's Physica: The Complete English Translation of Her Classic Work on Health and Healing* (Healing Arts Press: Canada, 1998)

Salvago, L., Umberto, A., *Was the English medieval goat genuinely rare? A new morphometric approach provides the answer* (Archaeological and Anthropological Sciences, 2019).

Simpson, J., Roud, S., *A Dictionary of English Folklore* (OUP: Oxford, 2003).

Skeat, W. W. (ed.), *The Vision of William Concerning Piers the Plowman, part 3* (Early English Text Society, Original Series 54, 1873).

Taylor, J. (ed.), *The Didascalicon of Hugh of St. Victor: A Medieval Guide to the Arts* (New York and London: Columbia University Press, 1961).

Toussaint-Samat,M., *A History of Food* (Wiley-Blackwell: Sussex, France, 2009)

Vehling, J., *De Re Coquinaria, or Apicius* (Walter Hill: 1936).

Warner, R. Rev., *Antiquitates Culinarie or Curious Tracts relating to the culinary affairs of the Old English* (London, 1791)

Willet Cummins, P., *A Critical Edition of Le Regime Tresutile et Tresproufitable pour Conserver et Garder la Santé du Corps Humain* (North Carolina Studies in the Romance Languages and Literatures: Chapel Hill, 1976).

Young, A., *Annals of Agriculture, Vol. 32* (J. Rackham: Bury St Edmunds, 1799).

Online Resources

An Anglo-Saxon Dictionary Online, bosworthtoller.com
British Newspaper Library, britishnewspaperarchive.co.uk
British Library, bl.uk/manuscripts
Koge Bog, forest.gen.nz/Medieval/articles/cooking/1616.html
Libellus De Arte Coquinaria, Wikipedia
Old English to Modern English Translator, oldenglishtranslator.co.uk
The Good Huswifes Jewell, medieval.com